100 MYTHS ABOUT THE MIDDLE EAST

Fred Halliday

100 MYTHS
ABOUT THE MIDDLE EAST

University of California Press
Berkeley   Los Angeles

3 9082 10463 8666

Published in the United Kingdom by
  Saqi Books,
  26 Westbourne Grove, London W2 5RH

Published in the United States by
  University of California Press,
  Berkeley and Los Angeles, California

Copyright © Fred Halliday 2005

Cataloging-in-Publication Data is on file with the Library of Congress

ISBN 0-520-24720-5 (case)
ISBN 0-520-24721-3 (paper)

Manufactured in Lebanon

14   13   12   11   10   09   08   07   06   05

10   9   8   7   6   5   4   3   2   1

'When I wished him a good trip and good luck in his new life, he replied with such typically Moslem phrases that I observed, "But you are Jewish. How is it that you speak of God in this manner?" His visage transfigured, he launched into a discourse of striking eloquence, and a crowd gathered around us. Only an *askari* looked disapproving and protested to me: "Why do you listen to this Jew?" I replied that everybody had the right to speak, and the majority of the crowd agreed with me. With astonishing oratorical ability for a simple peasant, the blacksmith proclaimed the glory of God, "Who is the same for all men", and "Who is present throughout the world".'

Claudie Fayein, *A French Doctor in the Yemen*, 1951

'Go into the London Stock Exchange ... there you will see the representatives of all nations assembled for the benefit of mankind. There the Jew, the Mohammedan and the Christian treat each other as if they were of the same religion, and they give the name of infidel only to those who are bankrupt.'

Voltaire, *Lettres Philosophiques*, 1728

'As best I could I had answered their many questions. They were surprised when I told them that Europeans were, with minor differences, exactly like them, marrying and bringing up their children in accordance with principles and traditions, that they had good morals and were in general good people.

"Are there any farmers among them?" Mahjoub asked me.

"Yes, there are some farmers among them. They've got everything – workers and doctors and farmers and teachers, just like us."

I preferred not to say the rest that had come to my mind: that just like us they are born and die, and in the journey from the cradle to the grave they dream dreams some of which come true and some of which are frustrated; that they fear the unknown, search for love and seek contentment in wife and child; that some are strong and some are weak; that some have been given more than they deserve by life, while others have been deprived by it, but that the differences are narrowing and most of the weak are no longer weak. I did not say this to Mahjoub, though I wish I had done so, for he was intelligent; in my conceit I was afraid he would not understand.'

Tayib Salih, *Season of Migration to the North*

Contents

Introduction

'We hear a lot about the roots of the Iberian Peninsula and of places beyond. We hear about the roots of our societies and historical communities … But man is not a tree. He does not have roots, he has feet, he walks.'

Juan Goytisolo, 'Metaforas de la migración', *El País*, 24 September 2004

In 1984 the British historians Eric Hobsbawm and Terence Ranger edited a book with the challenging title *The Invention of Tradition* (Cambridge University Press, 1992). In it, with a wealth of examples drawn from different countries, they showed how what is presented as a legacy of the past – as 'tradition' or 'heritage', as something given by history – is often a reflection of the contemporary imagination, an act of selection when not of invention. In the British Isles the modern 'family Christmas' and the Scottish kilt are examples of this, as is, in the years since the book was published, the celebration of St George's Day, 23 April, as an English national holiday and the prominence, not seen before in modern times, of the flag of St George itself.

The general significance of this book and of its central argument, is, however, enormous, since it goes to the heart of one of the most pervasive claims of modern times, of modern political culture and political ideology – that there is a given past, a set of established traditions, to which we in whatever country, culture and tradition can relate in both an analytic and a moral sense, i.e. which we can use to explain how the world is as it is, and also to provide a set of moral and sometimes religious principles, on the basis of which we can and should live. Such claims have, in many ways, become stronger in recent decades, in both the developed world – Europe, Japan and North America – and in the Third World, not least the Middle East. The most obvious form of this is the strengthening of claims based on interpretation of religious texts, what is generically and not wholly inaccurately termed 'fundamentalism', a trend evident in Islam, Judaism, Christianity and Hinduism. But the stronger claims of nationalism in general, across most of the world, also involve the invocation of the past, as something given and good. Whereas a generation or two ago, much was made of the campaign *against* the past, of the need to cast off the shackles of tradition, backwardness, superstition, obscurity in all its forms, in favour of a new aptly termed 'Enlightenment', we seem now to have reversed the argument. In politics, religion, customs, and, not least, food, the cult of the past, of the supposedly given and traditional, holds sway.

100 Myths about the Middle East is an attempt to engage with this trend, and rests on three broad arguments. The first is, in the spirit of Hobsbawm and Ranger, to question the historical accuracy of what is presented as the traditional and the authentic. The Middle East *appears* to be a region where the past, political, national and religious, holds sway – but on closer examination this is far from being the case. Whatever their claims to antiquity, all the states of the Middle East are modern creations, a result of the collapse of the Ottoman and Czarist Russian empires at the end of World War I, and of the interaction of these states with a modern global system of political, military and economic power.

When it comes to particular forms of claim and symbol, a similar modernity applies. Neither the claims of Islamist nor of Zionist politicians to be *recreating* a lost past are valid. The concept of the Islamic state, propounded in Shi'ism by Ayatollah Khomeini through the Iranian Revolution of 1978– 9, and that of a revived Caliphate, endorsed by conservative Sunnis including al-Qa'ida, are modern political projects. The state of Israel, for example, bears no relation except rhetorically to the ancient kingdoms of Solomon and David. Many of the most potent symbols of contemporary politics are also recent creations. Thus the Saudi monarchy's claim to be *khadim al-haramain* ('Servant of the Two Holy Places') was introduced only in 1986, and then in order to head off rival claims by King Hussein of Jordan to be the patron of the al-Aqsa mosque in Jerusalem; while Osama Bin Laden's comparable term for Arabia, *bilad al-haramain*, ('Land of the Two Holy Places') is an invention of his. All the monarchies of the Middle East claim ancient, ritualised, legitimacy, but they are, in fact, creations of the twentieth century, of the vogue for kingship that, late in the day, swept the Arab world, and, not least, of attentive, and at times military, support given to them at times of crisis by their more powerful friends in Europe and the US.

Much is made of the ancient, atavistic, millennial character of the Arab-Israeli conflict. This is pretext, and a misleading one at that – the causes of the contemporary Arab-Israeli conflict lie in the formation of two rival social and ethnic communities in Mandate Palestine in the period from 1920. They have nothing – except in the selective use of symbolism – to do with the texts of supposedly sacred books or events of 1,000, 2,000 or 3,000 years ago.

The conflict provides, indeed, good examples of how symbols are created and charged with modern meaning; of how, in effect, tradition can be invented. The two most potent visual symbols of Jewish identity are the *menorah* or seven-pronged candelabra, and the six-pointed star, known as the Star of David (*magen david*; literally, 'Shield of David' in Hebrew), the symbol on the Israeli flag. The *menorah* certainly is an ancient symbol of Jewish identity, but the Star of David is nothing of the kind: as a mystical symbol of the unity of mankind, it was for centuries used by Christians, Muslims and Jews and is to be found today on many mosques in Iran and the Persian Gulf area. It was only at the end of the nineteenth century that it was given this particular status, when adopted by the Zionist movement, and has nothing, in religion or history, to do with King David.

On the Palestinian side, perhaps the most prominent symbol is the checkered headdress worn by the late Yasser Arafat and adopted by supporters of Palestine across the world; it is derived from a military headdress designed by a Manchester trading house – itself of Syrian origin – in the 1920s, for the newly created Arab Legion force in Jordan. The same historical correction can be made for many elements of Turkish and Iranian nationalism. That these symbols and terms acquire meaning and are used to consolidate political power, if not to kill, is indisputable. But their impact, including the ability to kill, is given not by the weight of history but by modern political choices, emotions and purposes.

The second aim of this book is to challenge the assumption on which much contemporary discussion of religion, culture and civilisation is based, namely that in looking at religions or cultures we are looking at separate, discrete and monolithic entities. There are obviously distinct cultures in this world, as there are distinct languages and ethnic types, but they are far from being closed and have, over time, interacted creatively as well as antagonistically with each other. Much of what is supposedly 'European' comes from other places, and is nonetheless European for that: the dominant – but never sole – religion in Europe derives from events in Palestine two millennia ago; the scripts and mathematics of Europe have a similar Middle Eastern provenance; the languages of Europe, including in regard to domestic matters such as food and sex, bear a Middle Eastern imprint. How much of European food comes from Europe is another matter too – without tea, coffee, the potato, rice, the tomato and sundry fruits, herbs and spices, we would be left with a pretty miserable gruel indeed. The same is true of literature: the great writers of all nations, like Shakespeare and Cervantes, drew on other cultures, stories, motifs. At the Frankfurt Book Fair in 2004, dedicated to Arab literature, the Egyptian novelist Naguib Mahfuz argued that Arab literature drew on three great sources of inspiration: pre-Islamic poetry and told tales, Islamic culture and modern Western literature. So it has always been. The history of peoples is not national but cosmopolitan; not one, as nationalist myth would have us believe, of separate blocs gradually and belligerently getting to know each other, but of a constant process of cultural and commercial interaction, redefinition of boundaries and mutual enrichment. This is true today, in an age of globalisation, hybridity and 'world music', but was true centuries and millennia ago.

The third argument of this book is an ethical one, an assertion of the need – despite the current grovelling before tradition, the past, the authentic which besets us – to take a critical distance from this identification with history. The critical, historically sceptical perspective on myth, symbol and language is all the more important because, in many ways, these elements of public life have become more, not less, important in the contemporary world. Far from the world being swept by a wave of rationality, historical accuracy and universality, the very turmoil produced by globalisation, by the collapse and discrediting of the dominant radical ideologies of the twentieth century, of left and right, and by a world where violence in many and unexpected forms is prevalent, has led to a strengthening of myth and emotional claims. We are aware, through the work of sociologists and students of nationalism, of the role of such myths in mobilising people and enabling them to make sense of their complex and often bewildering lives. Hence we can recognise that the more rapidly the world changes, and the more interaction and conflict there are between peoples, the more potent these ideas become. That they are true or false, historically or linguistically accurate or not, is unimportant compared to the uses to which they are put, and the emotions with which they are upheld. All the more need, then, for some informed, measured doubts about such ideas and claims.

It is against this background that the following book has been compiled. Its purpose is, in a necessarily partial and at times haphazard way, to address these questions in regard to one particular region, the Middle East, and with a focus on two components of this debate: claims about the history of the region itself and the uses to which language is put, both by people in the region itself and by those relating to it from outside, the latter with a particular focus on changes and innovations in vocabulary since 11 September. It makes no claims to being comprehensive, definitive or even-handed. It is based on a reassertion of a critical view of claims about history and language, and on the relevance of what, in another context, I have termed 'international reason' – that is, a belief in a set of shared criteria, analytical and moral, for assessing international relations and in the power of rational argument to evaluate claims made by political, nationalist and religious forces about the contemporary world.

This book is part of a broader project of research and publication on the critique of national and religious thinking and the reconstitution of a theory of cosmopolitanism and internationalism, generously funded by the Leverhulme Trust, and which will hopefully lead to further works on issues of political theory and of contemporary international relations At the same time, it draws on both the main bodies of work that I have written in recent years: on one hand, a set of studies of the modern Middle East and its conflicts; on the other, the development of a set of ideas about world politics and, in particular, about the role of international theory in analysing them.

My central concern in both areas is to develop an argument as to how 'international reason', shorn of its determinist and monolithic aspirations but resolute in opposition to particularism, claims of national and religious authority and general rhetorical muddle, can help to understand and provide a moral vocabulary for discussing the contemporary world. We certainly need it, in the Middle East and elsewhere. In this way it is hoped that this book will contribute, beyond helping to cast light on particular events and ideas, to promoting a more informed and confident reassertion of cosmopolitan and internationalist thinking in the contemporary world.

100 MYTHS
ABOUT THE MIDDLE EAST

1

The Middle East is, in some fundamental way, 'different' from the rest of the world and has to be understood in terms distinct from other regions.

This idea is to be heard as often in the Middle East, where people are prone to vaunting their exceptionalism, as it is in hostile discussions in the West. If it is supposed to mean that there are distinct languages, religions, cuisines and customs in the Middle East this is indeed the case, but one that can only be made if it recognises the enormous differences between Middle Eastern societies and states themselves as much as between the region and the rest of the world. However, if it is meant to mean that the forms of social and political behaviour found in the region are somehow unique or cannot ·be explained in broad analytic terms used for other parts of the world, the claim is false. The main institutions of modern society – state, economy, family – operate in the Middle East as they do elsewhere. The modern history of the region, conventionally dated from 1798 – the French occupation of Egypt – is very much part of the broader expansion of European military, economic and cultural power in modern times, and has to be understood in broad terms comparable to the experience of other subjugated and transformed areas of the non-European world – Africa, Latin America, South Asia and East Asia.

The main features of Middle Eastern society to which those claiming its exceptionalism draw attention – dictatorship, rentier states, national-religious ideologies, subordination of women – are by no means specific to it. Of course, political actors in the region, be they conservative monarchies or radical Islamists, like to proclaim their originality and uniqueness, but this is part of the drive for political legitimacy, not a historical or analytic statement. If the region is supposed to be unique because of the impact of oil on its economies and societies, a brief study of other oil-producing states such as Indonesia, Nigeria, Venezuela and, above all in recent years, Russia and the former Soviet republics, will soon dispel any such illusion. If it is said to be unique because of the ferocity of its inter-ethnic conflicts, particularly the Arab-Israeli dispute, this too does not survive any comparative judgement: far more people have been killed in inter-ethnic conflicts in Rwanda, the former Yugoslavia and, be it not forgotten, twentieth-century central Europe, than in the more than half-century of the Palestine question.

Terrorism, too, is by no means peculiar to Islam or the Middle East; within the modern history of the region all religions have been used for purposes of mass murder and ethnic discrimination – as Jewish underground groups like Lehi and Irgun demonstrated in the 1940s, and as the Christian Maronites showed in Lebanon in the 1970s and 1980s. Elsewhere in the world, not to forget one of the historic proponents of terrorism along with the Irish and Bengalis in the nineteenth century and beyond, were the Christian Armenians. That particular bane of the 2000s, suicide bombings, were first pioneered by the (Hindu) guerrillas of Sri Lanka, the Liberation Tigers of Tamil Eelam. All regions, religions and peoples, like individuals, are in some ways unique in origin and characteristics; but characteristics shared with others are far greater by degree than those which distinguish. It is for this very reason that states, peoples and demagogues from all directions make such efforts to exaggerate their own, and their enemies', singularity.

The Middle East therefore shares far more with the rest of the world than it exhibits differences: all its societies, states and peoples are part of a world economy and subject to its changes; all uphold principles of national independence and culture and reject what they see as alien impositions; all protest when they are not accorded the rights and respect that the modern world, rightly, proclaims as being universal entitlements.

Beyond all of this, its peoples share the human emotions common to all mankind. In the words that Shakespeare wrote for his Jewish character Shylock in *The Merchant of Venice*: 'If you prick us, do we not bleed?' It is here, in the need and demand for universal respect and for a just place in the modern world, that the greatest source of anger and confusion in the Middle East resides – not in some supposed singularity, irrationality or peculiarity of religion, race or region. The roots of so-called 'Arab Rage' lie not in some purported cultural or religious pecularity of the Arabs, but in the adherence by the peoples of the Arab world to the universal claims of justice and equality which the rest of the world has propagated these two centuries past, and has now largely taken for granted.

2

The Middle East is a region dominated by hatred and solemnity; its peoples have no sense of humour.

Such things are not quantifiable; there is no UN Global Intercultural Hilarity Index. But my own impression, based on having visited several other regions of the world, including Eastern Europe, North and South America and East Asia, is that the peoples of the Middle East are less thin-skinned, more able to laugh about their rulers, their neighbours and themselves, than those of any other part of the world. You can spend weeks in Western Europe or the US without ever hearing a political joke, whereas in the Middle East no conversation, party or meeting with a friend in a café is complete without some anecdote, *nokta* (Arabic: 'joke'; literally, 'point') or report of the indiscretions of the powerful, real or imagined.

There are long traditions of such story-telling and jokes,

some involving complex linguistic and literary variations and puns, in several Middle East countries – notably featuring Mullah Nasruddin in Iran and Nasrettin Hoca in Turkey. Jewish culture has its own long traditions and styles of humour, although with Zionist Jews, as with other peoples the world over who have become devotees of nationalism (the Irish being another case in point), this tradition has been eroded in recent times. Israeli humour, while bitter and literary in its own way, pales before that of the Jewish diaspora. However, the very discredit in which so many Middle Eastern rulers are held means that jokes about and against them abound, much as they did in Eastern Europe under Soviet communism. Many of these stories are of an unprintable kind, involving lecherous *mullahs*; donkeys; the more outrageous claims of religious authorities be they *mullahs* or rabbis; personal hygiene; and the IQ of sons of incumbent presidents, if not of the presidents themselves. All of this, and more, is explored in a fine book by Khalid Qishtayni, *Arab Political Humour*.

In Iran, one of many examples of popular humour could be seen in Tehran in the summer of 1979, just after the revolution: at traffic lights little boys would be selling the usual oddments – chewing gum, shoe polish etc – but they also offered something else, a little volume titled *Kitab-i shukhi-yi ayatollah khomeini* ('The Ayatollah Khomeini Joke Book'). This turned out to be a selection of Khomeini's most preposterous writings on sex, hygiene and all matters personal and intimate. Another case of such anti-authoritarian Iranian irony came in 1989 with the controversy over

Salman Rushdie's novel *The Satanic Verses*. The novel, which includes a satirical treatment of the early history of Islam, was denounced by Khomeini and became the subject of an international controversy. No right-thinking supporter of the Islamic Republic could be seen to indulge such a tome. But an Iranian opposition group, knowing well the suspicious and imaginative propensities of the people, and precisely in order to attract a wider audience, started a new radio station called 'The Voice of *The Satanic Verses*'. Years later I met an Iranian man, a merchant from a provincial town on his first visit to the West. 'Please tell me,' he said, 'what did dear Mr Rushdie say? It must have been something great, because he annoyed those stupid *mullahs* so much!'

3

The incidence of war in modern times in the Middle East is a continuation from earlier times of violence and conquest, and of a culture that promotes violence.

The incidence of war in the post-1945 period has nothing to do with the earlier incidence of wars, or with a 'culture of conflict' inherited from pre-modern times. States, warriors and propagandists make much of such continuity, be it the Israelis invoking the warrior-king David, Saddam Hussein the Battle of Qadissiya or the Turks their conquering sultans; but this is symbolic usage, not historical explanation. As for there being a 'culture of violence' in the Middle East, this is a nebulous phrase that is almost without analytic purchase: certainly there are values and practices in these societies, such as parading small boys with guns and holding pompous military revues, that are usable for militaristic mobilisation and indoctrination, but so are there in other cultures – notably those of the former imperial powers of Europe, the US and Japan. The history of Europe in the twentieth century, and the brutality visited by some of its rulers on their own peoples, far outstrips anything seen in the modern Middle East.

4

Middle Eastern peoples have a particular sense of 'history', their own great part in it at some point in the past, their more recent humiliations and the need to prove themselves in terms of it.

Throughout the Middle East there is frequent reference to, and use of, 'history' to explain and justify current activities and events. However, according to any plausible criteria of the instrumentalised past, such a use and abuse of history is found just as much in other parts of the world – for example, the Balkans, Ireland, East Asia, Russia – as in the Middle East. Moreover, as with religious texts and traditions, the invocation of history reflects not the real effect of the past on the present, but the ransacking, selection and, where appropriate, invention of an ever-powerful history to justify current concerns. 'History' is here not a form of explanation, but of ideology.

5

Social behaviour, including attitudes to power, can be explained in terms of a distinctive, identifiable mindset, of all Arabs or Muslims or, more frequently, of Egyptians, Iraqis, Saudis, Turks and their various specific counterparts.

All peoples, and the politics and population of each modern state, have some distinct elements of political culture. Moreover, every state and society requires there to be certain values necessary for the sustenance of that system. But this is distinct from claiming some specific national 'mindset' based on ethnic, historically essentialist and too often stereotyped characteristics attributed to a people. Many of the 'special' attributes assigned so easily to one people or another, often by representatives of those peoples themselves, are shared with other peoples. A parallel process is latent in the often-made assertion as to some saying, folk wisdom or phrase supposedly embodying the uniqueness and history of a particular people: on closer, and comparative, inspection these nearly always turn out to be local variants of much wider, if not universal, observations.

6

Different European nations have 'special' relations to the Arab world and/or Middle East – e.g. the English, Greeks, Spanish, Germans, Irish …

The claim of some 'special' relation to the region is found in almost every European country with the exception of the Netherlands, which famously avoided the region by circumnavigating Africa. The Greeks, for example, like to present themselves as the *yefira* ('bridge') between Europe and the Arab world. The English hold onto some historical idea of their empathy for the desert Arab. The French make much of their involvement of more than a century with North Africa (*le Maghreb*), an association reflected in the presence of many Arabic words in contemporary spoken French – e.g. *baraka* for 'good luck', *bled* for 'countryside', *flouze* for 'money', *truchement* from the Arabic for 'translator', the equivalent of the English 'Dragoman' and *niquer* from the Qur'anic term for sexual relations. The Germans, who sought an alliance with Ottoman Turkey against the British, French and Russians before World War I, portray themselves as free of the colonialist associations of their British, Italian and French counterparts. The Spanish, who refused to recognise Israel until after the death of the fascist dictator Francisco Franco in 1975, make much of their own historic links to the Islamic world. But all of this is piety, when not a cover for commercial promotion. In modern times no European state has made good relations with the Muslim or Arab worlds a special priority and all have – as a function of imperial and post-imperial strategy, not endemic anti-Muslim sentiment – taken territorial and other advantage of them. All have, moreover, without exception, been pusillanimous and evasive on the rights of the Palestinian people.

7

The Arabs are a desert people.

This was not true in the seventh century, and is not true now. Indeed, the whole perception of the Arab world through the desert and its nomadic inhabitants is a grotesque distortion of the reality of these societies. One version of this is the use made by Arab and Western scholars of the theories of the mediaeval Tunisian writer Ibn Khaldun (1332–1406), through which these analysts seek to apply the conclusions about North African nomadic society (in its own time very brilliant) in his *Muqaddimah* or *Prolegomena* to the contemporary Arab world as a whole. This is like using an account of seventeenth-century English rural life to explain modern Britain. A more contemporary and self-serving version is the image portrayed of the Arab world by writers such as T. E. Lawrence, St John Philby, Wilfred Thesiger and others, the stock-in-trade of English travel writing about the Arabian Peninsula. These men may have been valiant and courageous explorers, but they tell us very little about the society of the modern Arab world, or even about the Arabian Peninsula; most people in the Peninsula are not nomads, but are either agricultural labourers (Yemen, Oman) or inhabitants of the eight or so major maritime and cosmopolitan cities that mark the coast of the Peninsula, from Kuwait City in the northeast via Manama, Dubai, Muscat, Mukalla, Aden and Hodeida to Jeddah in the southwest.

One further contributing factor to this myth may be the confusion which surrounds two potent but ill-defined words: 'desert' and 'tribe'. Strictly speaking, 'desert' refers to somewhere where nothing grows, in which case it accounts for only a quarter of the Arabian Peninsula, but it in conventional usage it also covers areas of land which should be more accurately termed as steppe, semi-arid land, brushland or thornland. Equally the association of Arabs with the 'desert' is assisted by mixing together the distinct categories of 'nomad', 'bedouin' (who may be settled) and 'tribe', this latter term being equally applicable to settled peasants or modern city dwellers. (See also Myth 88.)

8

The hostility of Arabs to Israel is a continuation of the hostility of European anti-Semites, especially the Nazis, towards the Jewish people.

The Arab and Muslim worlds were, *compared to Europe,* the scene of relatively less hostility to Jews in the centuries prior to the twentieth. It was, after all, to the Ottoman Empire to which the Jews expelled from Spain (known as *Sephardim,* from the Hebrew word for Spain), had fled in the late fifteenth and early sixteenth centuries. There was prejudice on religious and social grounds, but this was varied with time and country (see Myth 9). The rise of modern anti-Semitism as an ideology in Europe, from the mid-nineteenth century onwards, had virtually no impact on the Arab world for many decades and, even then, only through certain particular political parties and individuals. It was only after World War II, following the first Palestine war and the creation of Israel accompanied by the expulsion of hundreds of thousands of Palestinians, that anti-Semitism – now drawing on imported European themes – became strong in the Arab world. Over time a composite ideology, combining the themes of European anti-Semitism (in themselves confused) with specific Islamic themes, and hostility to the state of Israel and its policies as such, was formed.

9

There can be no 'anti-Semitism' in the European sense in the Middle East because both Arabs and Jews are Semites.

The word 'Semite', derived from Sham, one of the sons of Noah – and hence denoting all his putative descendants – technically covers all Jews and Arabs. But this claim, often pronounced with apparent solemnity in parts of the Arab world, is at best a play on words, at worst an evasion of responsibility. The term 'anti-Semitism', coined in the 1870s, means not hostility to all the possible descendants of Sham, in which case it would refer to Arabs as well, but rather prejudice against Jews.

The argument on the Arab/Muslim record towards Jews over the centuries is itself a battlefield of simplification on both sides: first, there is no single pattern of treatment of Jews and, as in Europe, periods of apparent tolerance were interrupted by bursts of violence, with or without official approval – it is therefore necessary to be specific about which country and time are being discussed; secondly, and beyond any doubt, the overall record of Muslim societies towards Jews is far superior to that of Europe over the past millennium, particularly in the twentieth century; as for the religiously-based criticisms of Jews found in Qur'anic passages, these were more often ignored than acted on, and pale in word and consequence before those of Christianity, with its claims (only formally renounced at the end of the twentieth century) of Jewish collective and eternal responsibility for the death of Jesus Christ.

10

On 11 September 2001, large numbers of Jews – sometimes said to be up to 4,500 – deliberately stayed away from the area of the World Trade Center towers in New York. They had, it was widely suggested, been warned to keep away, this indicating that there was some connection between the Israeli secret services and the al-Qa'ida hijackers.

This urban myth, in itself preposterous, was widely diffused on the Internet after 11 September. There is no evidence for it whatsoever.

The most widely diffused set of fantasies and fake inferences about September 11 is probably that of the bestselling *9/11: The Big Lie* by the French author Thierry Meyssan (Carnot, 2002).

11

The level of media coverage of the Arab world has been significantly raised in recent years by the emergence of a new group of satellite TV stations, most notably al-Jazeera (based in Qatar), which have offered an independent, alternative source of news and discussion of Middle Eastern affairs.

The emergence of the satellite TV stations certainly marked a change in the character of Arab TV broadcasts, restricted hitherto to stilted news and discussion programmes and to censorship of issues domestic and international. The new satellite stations are not, however, the harbinger of a new, freer media, since they are all owned and controlled by Arab states, with their own specific interests. Thus they are content to take a radical line on nationalist issues such as Palestine or Iraq, and to allow some open discussion on safe issues, but when it comes to more sensitive questions a whole set of red lines apply, as they do to the domestic press, Arabic- or English-language; thus corruption; state finances; dynastic succession problems; the social conduct of younger princes and the shopping practices of younger princesses; the treatment of migrants, women or children; and freedom of religious or sexual expression are all banned topics.

Moreover, by posturing for a nationalist audience, these stations and their dynastic and unaccountable backers, often resort to demagogy, distortion and alarmism that, far from contributing to greater understanding of international issues, serve (as does the yellow press in Europe) to inflame and mislead. The media in any society reflects, and does not create, the values and priorities of that society; the Arab satellite stations, including al-Jazeera, have been no exception.

12

There is today one Arabic language, spoken from Iraq in the east to Morocco in the west.

What constitutes 'one' language is open to debate, but by any conventional linguistic criteria, most obviously that of mutual intelligibility in spoken form, there is not one but are several Arabic languages. The language of official proclamations and of the media, Modern Standard Arabic, is a distinctive form all its own and is common to all states, but nowhere does it correspond even approximately to the spoken forms, the latter varying enormously from Morocco to Egypt, Iraq and Yemen. Early modern Arab linguists recognised this and tried to accommodate the spoken and written in each country, but the intense atmosphere of nationalist and religious discussion over these questions has, in recent years, made it much more difficult to recognise this problem, let alone bring about solutions or changes. The result is a region dominated by a linguistic orthodox fiction, while in practice diglossia – the need to know two different languages, the spoken and the written or standard – prevails. (For discussion see Professor Yasir Suleiman, *The Arabic Language and National Identity: A Study in Ideology*, Georgetown University Press, 2003.)

13

With the spread of Islam and the Arabic language in the seventh century, the pre-Islamic languages of Arabia were extinguished.

This is a common claim in histories of Islam, and is found even in the writings of such historians as Marshall Hodgson and Maxime Rodinson. In fact, to this day, at least eight distinct pre-Arabian languages survive in spoken form along the South Arabian Coast, in the Dhofar province of Oman; in the Mahra province of Yemen; and on the island of Socotra. These languages, including Jabbali, Harrasis, Botahhari, Mahri and Socotri, are sometimes referred to by speakers as 'Himyari', as if directly descended from the language of the ancient Himyaritic Kingdom of Yemen, but this appears not to be the case. In recent decades linguistic experts have recorded, analysed and transcribed these South Arabian tongues.

14

Modern Standard Hebrew, the language used in Israel today, is a 'revival' of the Hebrew of Biblical times.

As with Arabic, Hebrew nationalism and religion reinforce a linguistic fiction. The first problem with the Jewish nationalist claim to be 'reviving' their language is that, long before the destruction of the Second Temple and the dispersal of the Jews in 70 AD, Hebrew had died out as a spoken language in Palestine, being replaced by Aramaic, a related Semitic language and the one spoken by Jesus Christ; this tongue survives to this day in some villages in Syria, east of Damascus.

Hebrew is not, therefore, 'the' but one of several languages of the Jews. Another modern Jewish tongue is Yiddish, a combination of German and Hebrew vocabulary written in Hebrew script which was the shared language of the Ashkenazi Jews of Eastern Europe and which modern Zionism has sought to repudiate. Still another is Ladino, a form of Spanish spoken by Sephardic Jews that has survived into modern times. Equally important is the language of the largest Jewish community in the world, Arabic; until well after the establishment of Israel in 1948, Arab Jews saw no contradiction in being Jewish in religion and/or culture and having Arabic as their mother tongue.

The language spoken today in Israel, Modern Hebrew, is for all intents and purposes and according to any reasonable linguistic criteria a different language to that of Biblical times – the latter known as *ivrit tanakhit* ('the Hebrew of the Tanakh', or Jewish Bible). Significantly, the revival of Hebrew was not part of the original Zionist programme: Theodor Herzl, in his programmatic *Der Judenstaat* ('The State of the Jews'), proposed that each community migrating to the Jewish State should retain its own language and suggested the model of Switzerland, where four languages have official recognition. However, the pioneer Zionist Eliezer Ben-Yehuda campaigned for the adoption of Hebrew, in line with the standard nationalist programme of 'reviving' ancient traditions, and produced a new form of the language. The grammar was fundamentally revised, and much of the vocabulary was either invented using Hebrew roots or taken from other contemporary Semitic languages.

The new Hebrew succeeded quickly, and was reinforced after 1948 by an official policy designed to make immigrants speak the language; public places in Israel after 1948 were decked with the slogan *ivrit, daber ivrit* ('Hebrew, Speak Hebrew'). The success of Hebrew appears overwhelming, and Yiddish and Ladino are dying; but change and challenge are not far away, as in recent years the large numbers of Russian – and in significant degree, gentile – immigrants have come to insist on retaining Russian as their language within Israel itself.

Moreover, the success of this new modern language created its own problems of diglossia, as with Arabic, because in line with the nationalist myth that the two languages were the same, children in the diaspora were taught 'Hebrew' (by which was implied the language of Israel today) when in fact what they were being taught was the classical variant – as if a student of Italian were being taught Latin.

The example of Hebrew may have benefited the Jewish community in Israel, but it is certainly part of a nefarious wave across the world, where disproportionate and too often introverted campaigns for linguistic revival and assertion have sprouted across the twentieth century – in Ireland, for example, or Euzkadi (the Spanish Basque country). Even in the Canary Islands, on the basis of what are said to be 250 known words from an earlier pre-Spanish language called Guanche, a revival movement arose in the 1970s with, inevitably, the slogan *Patria Guanche o Muerte, Venceremos* ('Our Homeland, Guanche or Death: We Shall Prevail'). (The name of the Canary Islands derives literally from their Latin name 'The Dog Islands'; they are claimed by some Arab nationalists as *Juzur al-Qumr*, 'The Moon Islands', also the origin of the name of the most unknown of all Arab states, the Comoros, in the Indian Ocean.) The cost of all this linguistic obsession, in a world where the cultural and economic, let alone human, imperative is to learn major tongues, has yet to be calculated.

15

Kurdish is understood as the language spoken by the 40 million or so Kurds who live in Iran, Iraq, Turkey and Syria. Here, too, nationalist ideology and the political claim that the Kurds are 'one' people, rest on the assertion that there is 'a', or 'one' Kurdish language.

The reality of linguistic diversity and mutual unintelligibility once again collides with nationalist aspiration. According to reasonable linguistic criteria there are at least two distinct, mutually unintelligible Kurdish languages, Kirmanji and Sohrani, with many dialects. The denial of such linguistic diversity compounds the major problem that, far from being in any social or political sense 'one' people, the Kurds of Iran, Iraq and Turkey are organised in distinct ways, with different traditions and, most importantly, very different contemporary political aspirations. The 'failure' to achieve a united independent Kurdistan is thus a reflection not of some political weakness of Kurdish leaders, or oppressive character of the states in which they live, but of the fact that in politics and society, as in language, no 'one' Kurdish nation exists. This is not to deny that such a single Kurdish nation could come into existence in the future, but the reality is, to date, very different.

16

In the case of the other main linguistic group in the region, the opposite nationalist myth prevails, one of bogus distinctiveness. Here it is claimed that in contradistinction to the Persian spoken in Iran, there are separate languages in the neighbouring states of Afghanistan (Dari), and in the former Soviet republic of Tajikistan (Tajik).

The fiction of linguistic unity, evident in Arabic, Kurdish, Hebrew and Berber, contrasts with that of linguistic separation. An evident recent case of this is the claim, preposterous to all who know about Yugoslavia, that what was previously one language (Serbo-Croat), although written in two distinct scripts and with some small variations in vocabulary, is now not two but *three* different languages – Serbian, Croatian and, for Bosnia, Bosniak. In the case of Persian and its variants, the claim that Afghan Dari (literally, 'of the house', meaning the language of the Persian-speaking Mohammadzai dynasty, which ruled until 1973), is a distinct language meets neither the test of unintelligibility or vocabulary. BBC broadcasts to Iran and Afghanistan use the same spoken language. There are differences of vocabulary (e.g. for 'hospital', instead of the Persian *bimarestan* Afghans say *shafakhane*, with the same root as the Arabic *mostashfa*. There are also slight variations in forms of verbal abuse, Persians preferring *pedarsag* ('son of a dog'), while Afghans prefer *laanat bi pedar* ('curses on your father'); but these are no greater than between American and Australian English on one side and British English on the other. Some of the greatest Persian poetry is by writers from today's Afghanistan (Rumi) or Tajikistan (Ferdousi), as well as now-Azeri speaking Azerbaijan (Nizami).

17

The politics of the Middle East are governed by a set of rules peculiar to this region.

There are no such 'special rules' shaping the Middle East or any other region. The forces determining Middle Eastern politics over the past two centuries have been those of an expanding, militarised and economically ever more powerful, developed Western world. Relations between Middle Eastern states are, beneath the carapace of fraternity and equality that is found elsewhere in the world as well, governed by calculations of states, factional interests within states, balances of internal and external state calculation and, to some degree, ideology. If there are 'rules', tendencies, iterations, they are part of a broader pattern of international and regional state behaviour.

18

The 'West' has, for centuries, been hostile to 'Islam'.

Unless contextualised, there is little meaningful sense in which the term 'West' can be used to denote a political process taking place over centuries. Nor can the term 'Islam', beyond some common religious beliefs and a shared sense of injustice, have much political purchase either. Once analysed on the basis of specific states and policy issues no coherent pattern emerges and, indeed, there have been many cases since 1600 of alliances between European/US policies on the one side and those of particular Middle Eastern states on the other. The claim of trans-epochal confrontation is a political convenience and myth on both sides, and nonetheless effective for being that.

The very categories in which this argument has been made are mistaken. There is no one 'West', nor has there ever been one, while Islam, in the sense of Islamic states and political forces, has always been plural and has been much more so with the emergence of over fifty Muslim states after World War II. Three more specific points: first, the state formation and identity development of European states were not, despite many claims to this effect, shaped by the encounter with the Islamic 'Other' but through interaction with each other, as well as through internal, political and economic change; secondly, the European states interacted in a flexible, often competitive manner with the Ottoman Empire in the nineteenth century and up to World War I, without any set hostility or exclusion; finally, the more than fifty Islamic states of the world today have no uniform pattern of relations with the West: they range from close economic and/or strategic alliances to hostility and confrontation, the latter resting not on religious orientation or piety but on clashes of state and national interest.

19

We live in an age when international relations are dominated by a 'clash of civilisations'.

This is a thesis popularised by the American writer Samuel P. Huntington in a book published in 1996. Its theme has been enthusiastically taken up by fundamentalists and nationalists, not only in the Muslim world but in India, Russia and Japan as well. No one can deny that issues of culture, identity and, more broadly, 'civilisation' play a role in relations between peoples and states. This has, however, been the case for centuries and indeed millennia, as the wars of religion and the role of culture in the development of modern popular identity and worldview, i.e. what has been known since around 1780 as 'nationalism', demonstrate. There are certainly issues of culture in contemporary political debates, as questions of immigration, inter-ethnic conflict and linguistic campaigning illustrate. But culture was never historically the dominant factor, as the wars between Christian states and Islamic states themselves show, nor is it today. The bloodiest Middle Eastern war by far was that between Iran and Iraq (1980–8) in which over a million people are believed to have died.

20

Since the end of the Cold War, the West, having lost an enemy in communism, has now invented another one in Islam, hence the rise of hostility to Islam and Muslims, what is termed 'Islamophobia'.

The term 'Islamophobia', now in general usage and accepted by governments and police forces as a term with legal relevance, is a misnomer propagated in the early 1990s by Muslim groups within Western society seeking to legitimate their own social position *vis-à-vis* non-Muslim society, and ideological position *vis-à-vis* their own Muslim communities. Hostility to Islam as a religion, common in earlier centuries, is relatively rare now: there are few books for sale arguing that Muhammad was a fraud, or similar claims. Contemporary prejudice is against Muslims as people, and should properly be termed not 'Islamophobia' but 'anti-Muslimism'.

Appeals to such supposed 'deep', 'structural' or even 'tectonic' forces in world affairs are very successful but, on closer examination, fall apart. 'Islam' is not, in any realistic sense, a political or social alternative to Western liberal democracies, as communism was, nor – for all the effects past and to come of 'mega-terrorism' – does it pose a strategic military threat as the USSR certainly did, with 40,000 nuclear weapons and several million men under arms in Europe. Beneath these facts lies, however, the most questionable myth of all, namely that in some plausible way the West 'needs' an enemy. The logic of capitalism is, rather, that a peaceful world in which countries trade and peacefully compete with each other is the most desirable. Alarmist and amateur meta-historical psychoanalysis is no substitute for substantive explanation specifying contexts and events. Apart from fuelling despondency in the West, this argument also makes Islamists feel good, as they can claim to be taking up the mantle of challenging 'the West' now that communism has failed in the task: this, too, is claptrap.

21

The politics of Middle Eastern states need to be understood to a large degree, perhaps totally, in terms of the workings of 'conspiracies', unseen agendas, plots, 'hands', arrangements, fixings and long-sighted manipulations on the part of alien, usually Western, powers.

Plots and conspiracies there most certainly have been in the past two centuries of Middle Eastern politics, and we can be sure there will be more. Yet the reliance on such ideas reflects two major problems: first, a resort to mythical analysis instead of substantive, evidence-related argument; second, a denial, underlying virtually all conspiracy theories, of the at least partial role and responsibility of local forces and actors in the outcome of events. Far from being a revelation of external cause, this mindset is itself a trap, not only inaccurate and mythical but a reflection and reinforcement of paralysis. This is evident from what is, again, necessary when faced with any supposed singularity, which is comparison. Conspiracy theory is evident in many countries, including China and Serbia, and has a long pedigree in the US, where nativist and paranoid political themes are recurrent if not prevalent. The speculation that has lasted for decades after the assassination of President John F. Kennedy is one instance of this: at one point, such theories were so popular that a telephone service in Chicago provided a line, revised every day, called 'Dial-a-Conspiracy'.

22

The crisis of the Arab world can be explained by the negative impact of the conflict with Israel on democratisation and social change.

The Israel-Palestine conflict has certainly reinforced the authoritarian character of the states immediately adjacent to them – Egypt, Jordan, Lebanon and Syria (although relations between Israel and the first two of these states have become normalised, if not wholly cordial). In the case of Lebanon, by way of invasion and occupation by Israel from 1982, the conflict exacerbated already existing and growing internal hostilities.

The Arab-Israeli conflict is at best a partial explanation, and at times nothing more than a pretext, for the persistence of authoritarian rule. It says nothing about the reasons for the predominance of kleptocratic family and political elites, the misuse of oil revenues, the prevalence of conservative religious censorship, the denial of the rights of workers and women or the poor quality of education.

However, Arab regimes have tended to use the 'urgent priority' of the conflict with Israel as a fig leaf to deflect criticism aimed at the more repressive and undemocratic aspects of their governments.

23

The contemporary Middle Eastern state can be explained in terms of institutions, traditions and cultures derived from 'Asiatic', 'Oriental despotic' or other earlier regional forms of state.

Middle Eastern states have a long history of despotism and apparent socioeconomic stagnation, but this is not directly relevant to the region as transformed, since 1800 or thereabouts, by international modernity. The authoritarian character of the modern state is a result of recent institutional formation, the domestic and international forces acting on it and the ability of the ruling elites to use coercive, economic and ideological resources to remain in power – helped, in ways large and small, visible and not so visible, by their international friends.

24

Middle Eastern societies are marked, despite the appearance, pretence or official simulation of change, by an underlying stasis of social, political, even economic forms of behaviour which make the region exempt from many of the changes seen elsewhere during the course of modern times – in particular, the twentieth century.

The greatest mistake in the analysis of the contemporary Middle East is to assume continuity and a lack of change in social, political and economic processes. Even when continuity can or may be shown, e.g. in forms of belief or the status of religious authorities, this continuity and reproduction itself needs explanation. In general, and in contrast to images of a timeless 'Oriental despotic' impasse, a timeless and hypostatised 'Arab Mind', or the enduring effectivity of a monist and often fetishised 'Islam', the modern world has brought and continues to bring enormous change to Middle Eastern societies even as those proposing or militating for change cloak this in a mask of continuity or 'return' to the past.

25

Arab economic and political backwardness is explained by the desire of the West to ensure subjugation of Middle Eastern societies and economies in order to extract and control oil in a manner favourable to them.

In regard to the re-appropriation by the West of oil revenues, the investment of these in Western economies is a function of the local states' security concerns and inability to develop their economies, not of some Western financial-security strategy.

26

Oil has been and may become even more of a source of conflict in the modern Middle East.

Middle Eastern oil has been, and will remain, a major source of concern for strategic, commercial and now environmental reasons. It has aroused widespread nationalist protest. Through the socioeconomic changes associated with the inequalities and corruption of the rentier state it has, as in Iran in 1978–9, and Algeria since 1989, fuelled a growing social crisis that has erupted in political violence. But for all the wars and inter-state conflicts of the modern Middle East, oil has not yet been a subject of significant dispute between states.

27

The US, backed by the UK, invaded and occupied Iraq in 2003 to gain control of Iraqi oil.

If Washington had wanted to gain control of Iraqi oil, monopolising or effectively controlling its production and/ or distribution, it could have done so at much less expense of money and authority, by doing a deal with Saddam Hussein: the Iraqi dictator had always hoped to settle in an overall strategic deal with the US, and had kept his French and Russian interlocutors and potential oil partners at bay for that reason. The US and UK had a different agenda; cf. Myth 28.

28

The reason for the US-British invasion of Iraq in March 2003 was because Iraq had significant supplies of Weapons of Mass Destruction (WMD).

The claim that Iraq had significant stockpiles of WMD in early 2003, or that Washington or London seriously believed they did, was unfounded. The claim about WMD was made not because of 'faulty' intelligence, nor from any belief that Iraq still had major WMD potential, but as part of a policy of 'threat inflation' – common during the Cold War – used to justify actions that had quite different motives which Washington and London found it hard to articulate specifically – namely, a wish to reimpose strategic control on West Asia as a whole.

The attack on Iraq was not driven by any specifically economic interests, but more by a set of intermixed ideological concerns that had been promoted in Washington before Bush was elected in 2000 and which came to take hold in the upper leadership of his neoconservative administration. These included the wish to demonstrate American power to allies and foes alike, and the fantasy, fuelled by dogma and ignorance at the highest level and encouraged by the Israeli government, that the destruction of the Ba'thist regime in Baghdad would have wider and beneficial consequences in the region. Ironically, the Bush administration's decision-making process, secretive and elitist, was that normally associated with the dictatorial regimes of the Middle East; while the latter, for all their authoritarian powers and character, had always to take note of what their public opinion would and would not accept.

29

A significant reduction of world dependence on Gulf oil, and of the need to engage directly with the authoritarian rulers of that region, can be achieved through the development of new fields in the Caspian Sea region, particularly in Kazakhstan and Azerbaijan.

Ever since the emergence of independent oil economies around the Caspian Sea after the collapse of the USSR in 1991, there has been much talking up of the energy potential of the region, especially by those concerned with lessening the influence of Iran and/or the Gulf states on the world oil market. Western speculators, Iranian exiles and Russian oil entrepreneurs, as well as local states, have pushed this argument. There is significant oil and gas in and around the Caspian, more than was realised in Soviet times. But much of the publicity about the global potential of this oil is hype, for commercial or political reasons. First, even assuming all other problems are solved, the overall export potential of the Caspian Sea region as a whole by 2020 is reckoned to be 8 million barrels of oil a day – a significant amount, and equal to Saudi or Russian production, but not enough to replace the Gulf, let alone meet the expected increase in global demand by that date.

However, the region is beset by a range of political problems that are unlikely to be resolved in short order: the dispute between littoral states about whether the Caspian is a lake or a sea (which affects the allocation of drilling concessions); the unresolved conflict between Azerbaijan and Armenia over the enclave of Nagorno-Karabagh; the war in Chechnya, until now part of Russia; the presence in Georgia of separatist enclaves; the rivalry between Trans-Caucasian, Russian and Turkish interests; major human rights and environmental concerns about pipelines and maritime transport of oil. Even the building of a pipeline from Baku in Azerbaijan to Ceyhan in Turkey, thus bypassing Russian pipelines and ports has, while being pushed by the US for political reasons, encountered many obstacles. Exporting oil from the Gulf is, by contrast, simple: pipelines lie across a few hundred miles of flat land to the port, where the ships can dock or reach the open seas in a matter of hours. This dispute was summed up in a remark by a Saudi oil expert: the pro-Caspian oil companies had, in order to circumvent local and regional political rivalries, produced a bumper sticker with the words 'Happiness is Multiple Pipelines'. The Saudi reply? 'Happiness is No Pipelines!'

30

The new cause of conflict in the Middle East is going to be water, with the prospect of 'hydrowars', i.e. wars about water, looming in the future.

There are serious issues pertaining to water usage within contemporary Middle Eastern states, where demand is outstripping supply, and there are at least three regions where water issues are, or could well be, a source of conflict or even war: the Israel-Jordan-Syria triangle, over the tributary waters to the Jordan; the relation of the Nile states – Egypt, Sudan, Ethiopia – to that river; and the balance between Turkish water diversion and dam policies and the flow of the Tigris and Euphrates to Syria and Iraq. None of this, however, adds up to an inevitable prospect of wars over water, or to the return of environmental and resource allocation issues as sources of conflict, as was the case with water and grazing in primitive societies. Issues of water use *within* countries can be solved by the adoption of sensible policies, ones that in particular avoid using water for inappropriate agricultural schemes. The allocation of water *between* states is quite feasible *if there is political goodwill* between them: the source of the conflict lies in inter-state rivalry, not in the water as such. (See Tony Allan, *The Middle East Water Question: Hydropolitics and the Global Economy*, London, I. B. Tauris, 2001.)

31

Whatever other regional data may be unreliable, we can be sure of figures for Middle Eastern oil exports (normally expressed in terms of millions of barrels per day [mbd]) and oil revenues.

Statistics for national economies and social indicators are, the world over, far less precise than is generally claimed. Even for developed states, figures for, say, population, per capita income, consumption or unemployment show considerable ranges of imprecision and variation. When it comes to other states, all figures except the area of national territory are dubious.

With regard to oil, despite the convention of asserting a figure for daily output for each country it is possible to establish a precise output figure only two years after the event. Even then, there are at least four different ways of reaching a figure based on the methods of, respectively, the US Department of Energy, BP, *The Oil and Gas Daily* (Texas) and *Middle East Economic Survey* (Cyprus). As for oil imports, these are even harder to establish. When it comes to other, related, financial figures there is no reliable basis for calculation. Figures for annual oil revenues of states are often little more than informed guesses of budgets or international banks and financial institutions. As for the disposition of oil revenues, and the figures for revenue invested in Western markets and the revenues gained therefrom, no reliable statistics are available at all. On top of this comes the issue, of primary importance for evaluating the future of the world economy and appropriate investment needs, of oil reserves. Statistics for a country's reserves are regularly given and quoted but these are guesses, a product of national and oil-company politics on one hand and the state of exploration technology on the other.

32

The problem with the Middle East in the age of globalisation is that it is somewhat removed from the world economy, and needs further integration with it.

This is nonsense. In the first place, the world relies on the region for over a third of its current energy supplies, and is likely to do so for up to two-thirds of its needs by 2020, unless one or another of two most unlikely things happen – that major new supplies of oil are found elsewhere in the world or that a realistic and speedily introduced alternative is developed to the internal combustion engine.

Secondly, the revenues earned by Middle Eastern oil producers, and the funds acquired from these producers by other regional states in the form of loans, grants and remittances are, to a considerable but utterly unquantifiable degree, reinvested in the West, and contribute much to the stability of property and financial markets there. Estimates of Arab Gulf financial holdings in the West go as high as US$5 trillion. (By way of comparison, the US annual GDP is US$10 trillion.)

Thirdly, in other, more human respects, Europe itself is interlocked with the region: specifically, as a result of the failure of Middle Eastern – particularly North African – states to develop their economies, more and more Middle Eastern migrant workers are crossing the Mediterranean to work in Europe. The West, which owes its religions, some of its historical continuity with ancient Greece and Rome and a fair share of its eating habits and interior design aesthetics to the region, is, as it has been for more than two millennia, inextricably tied to the Middle East.

33

The condition of the Arab world is to be explained by the impact of traditional values and a 'failure' to respond to the modern world and its norms.

This became the favourite Western explanation for the condition of the Arab world in the 1990s and 2000s, and was the perspective that underlay the 2002 report by the United Nations Development Programme (UNDP) on the Arab world and the later US Greater Middle East Initiative, a short-lived public relations episode of 2004. Many of the phenomena referred to in the UNDP report, for example, were accurate, but they omitted the historical and international context in which these societies have been shaped, one or two centuries of subjugation to the West, the creation of authoritarian states and rentier economies and the moulding of these societies into unstable but subordinate formations.

34

The Middle East, since the early 1990s, under the influence of globalisation and the worldwide trend towards liberal economics and politics, has been characterised by a process of gradual liberalisation and incipient democratisation marked above all by the rise of 'civil society'.

This is, by any objective criteria for assessing either the openness of markets or the real transition to democracy, a fiction; it is wishful thinking on the part of the well-intentioned within the region and without, deliberate obfuscation and outright propaganda by states and their paid apologists designed to lull international opinion. The one country where there has been substantial economic and political progress towards liberalisation is Turkey, but even here ultimate power rests with the military, and abuses and denial of human rights continue on a systematic scale. In Israel, the democratic system has been increasingly held hostage to sectarian, calculating religious fanatics, even as the economy did become more liberalised. In Iran and the Arab world, there has been change, but of a limited and sometimes regressive character.

In some societies, a degree of limited freedom of expression and publication has been permitted, and in others the level of incarceration, torture and forced exile has declined. These are substantive and welcome developments. But on two other fronts, the balance has been different. First, none of the four core conditions of democratic order have applied: publicly available, accurate figures for state finances, income and expenditure; institutionalised and legally protected independent political parties; the ability of the electorate to vote out those with real power; full freedom of the press and information, within the legal limits set by international law. Secondly, while control by governments has continued, through overt and covert means (the latter sometimes including fake 'NGOs' – or, as they are known by the sceptical, 'GINGOs', Governmental NGOs), the political programmes and political culture of many of the opposition forces have themselves become increasingly undemocratic, dominated by programmes of religious and confessional authoritarianism.

35

The Arab states of the Gulf, such as Kuwait and Saudi Arabia, are 'feudal' in character.

This was a claim often made by radical Arab writers and by Western anti-imperialists in the 1980s and 1990s about the Gulf oil-producing monarchies, and was commonly used particularly by those who opposed the armed eviction of Iraq from Kuwait in 1990–1. The survival of patriarchal distributive regimes in these countries may not correspond to criteria of democracy, but these are thoroughly capitalist states, relying on the sale of their oil exports on the world market, trading domestically and internationally according to capitalist criteria and investing their surpluses in global financial, property and other markets.

36

The politics of the Middle East before and during modern times is the preserve of states, external powers and internal despotisms, without reference to the movements of peoples from below.

Nothing could be further from the truth. The whole history of the Muslim world is marked by popular revolts, spontaneous movements of peoples and the emergence of new social and ideological, religious but also ethnic and political, trends. In modern times, say, since the middle of the nineteenth century, the region has witnessed numerous popular movements – first in Iran and Egypt; then, after World War I, in most Arab states; then, after World War II, in the form of nationalist and communist, later Islamist, movements. Indeed, it is debatable whether the main narrative of modern Middle Eastern history is that of states at all.

37

There are no classes in the Middle East. The concept of 'class', and broader Marxist categories of social formation, world capitalist economy and the formation of exploitative states are irrelevant to understanding the region.

Marxists have worked for many years to provide an analysis of Middle Eastern society, its states and ideologies, including religion, which sets these phenomena in a historical and socioeconomic setting. Some of these analyses have been of a simplifying kind, as with many of the radical Arab and Iranian Marxist analyses of the 1960s and 1970s, but the more astute and theoretically able works within the Marxist tradition must count among the best writing on the region. Among these can be cited the works of Hanna Batatu, Ervand Abrahamian, Maxime Rodinson, Faleh A. Jabar and, in his early work, Bernard Lewis. 'Class analysis' must have acquired a bad name for oversimplification, such as trying to reduce the Iranian clergy to being a faction or other of the 'petty bourgeoisie', or searching for 'kulaks' and 'middle peasants' in Arab or Iranian society; but anyone with the slightest academic, let alone first-hand, knowledge of these societies will recognise that those with access to wealth and control of rent and production form a class as eager as any in the world to hold onto its privileges and keep those without such access at bay. As for the overarching context of Marxist analysis, the capitalist 'mode of production', this has been the dominant global and regional socioeconomic context for the Middle East for more than a century. The current dominant phase, globalisation, is the latest, if distinct, chapter in this process.

38

Islam does not allow for a separation of religion and politics, and hence of what in modern European thought is termed 'secularism'. This is evident from Islamic history, and is expressed in the Muslim saying *al-islam dinun wa dawlatun* ('Islam is a religion and a political system').

This is a retrospective, contemporary rationalisation of a much more complex story. The unity of religious and political power lasted in Islam less than a century, from the establishment of the Muslim state in Mecca in 632 AD to the death for the fourth *caliph* Ali in 661 AD. Thereafter, while all rulers used religious symbolism to legitimate their rule and in some cases claimed to be *sayyids*, or descendants of the Prophet, there existed a clear distinction between the political ruler, the sultan or king or other title, and the religious authorities, the *ulema*. Thus, in the last of the three major Islamic empires, the Ottoman, there was a sultan and a *seyh-ul-islam* (the highest religious authority), while in Saudi Arabia the ruling family of Al Saud has held temporal power, with (subordinate) religious power being in the hands of the Al Shaikh, the descendants of the founder of their religious movement, al-Wahhab. As for the saying '*al-islam dinun wa dawlatun*', this is not a classical Islamic formulation at all, neither a verse of the Qur'an nor a quote or *hadith* but a nineteenth-century political slogan popularised by the Salafi movement that emerged in opposition to Western influence in Egypt.

39

Middle Eastern economic performance today and, more generally, in history has to be seen in terms of the impact, the prescriptions and proscriptions of the region's religions.

Religion has no significant role in explaining economic history or, in the contemporary world, comparative economic performance. The earlier aspiration of social science, epitomised in Max Weber's analysis of the relationship between the spirit of Protestantism and the rise of capitalism, to explain economic growth in religious and doctrinal terms, and in the context of elective affinities or compatibilities between religion and economic activity, has been shown to be circular. As for Islam, it can in theory and has in practice legitimised a variety of socioeconomic forms, from slavery and pre-modern agrarian societies (loosely referred to as 'feudalism') to modern capitalism as in the Gulf and forms of state-direct socialism. Both the textual basis and the ideological orientation are available to those who wish, as in other matters of modernist instrumentalisation, to use the existing resources of a religion to legitimate their – in this case economic – activity. (The classic reference on this is Maxime Rodinson's *Islam and Capitalism*, University of Texas Press, 1978.) On 'Islamic economics' in particular, see the following Myth.

40

The solution to the problems of the Middle East lies in the application of *iqtisad-i islami*, or 'Islamic economics'.

There is no such thing as 'Islamic economics' any more than there is such a thing as 'Islamic banking', 'Islamic aeronautics' or 'Islamic mathematics'. This idea was particularly advocated during the Iranian Revolution by writers such as Abol-Hassan Banisadr, an advisor to Ayatollah Khomeini; Banisadr was, then, the first president of the Islamic Republic and, after July 1981, a refugee in France. Theoretically Islamic economics was a hodgepodge of populist and socialist ideas. In practice it amounted to nothing more than inefficient state control of the economy and some almost equally ineffective redistribution policies. In a political and regional context where Islamists and *ulema* claim to have an opinion about everything, it is striking how little they have to say about this most central of human activities, beyond repetitious pieties about how their model is neither capitalist nor socialist. The classical Islamic texts have nothing – repeat, nothing – of relevance to say on the matter beyond general – and, so far as they go, valid – exhortations to equity and redistribution in accordance with the principle of *zakat*, one of the five principal duties of every Muslim.

41

The Muslim religion enjoins its believers to abstain from involvement in Western banking and operate their own system of 'Islamic banking'. The involvement of Islamic societies and businessmen in finance is complicated by Islam's ban on the taking of interest, following the Qur'anic prohibition of *riba*. This requires the creation of a parallel, 'Islamic', banking sector, the growth of which has been noted in recent years, especially in Turkey, the Gulf and South Asia.

The Qur'anic injunction on *riba* (literally 'increase', arbitrarily rendered by some commentators as 'interest') has never, in practice, prevented Muslim financiers from charging and earning interest, nor, in modern times, from participating as investors and creditors in the international banking and financial systems. The recent growth in 'Islamic banking' has nothing to do with religious rules but is, rather, an attempt by an alternative, aspirant financial class in the Middle East and elsewhere to enter the market with a different brand image. Unofficial information from the Gulf also suggests that, given the reservations, not to say suspicions, of many local people about handing their money to Western banks, and, not least, the kinds of questions as to the origin of their funds this might occasion (not least after 11 September), there is a sense of greater confidence about 'local', Islamic, banks. 'It is a way of getting the stuff out from underneath people's floorboards and beds', was how one expert put it to me.

What may vary is not so much the principles, let alone practice, of borrowing and investing, but the forms of regulation to which the different banks are subjected. One of the first modern 'Islamic banks' was, of course, the ill-fated (for its investors, not its directors) Bank of Commerce and Credit International. There have also been serious problems regarding the honesty and solvency of Islamic financial institutions in Egypt. Elucidation of this matter, and in particular of the positive attitude of the Qur'an and the Islamic tradition to economic activity in general, trading, commercial profit, wage labour and so forth, is found in Maxime Rodinson's *Islam and Capitalism*. With regard to the definition of *riba* as 'interest', Rodinson writes: 'In any case, the results arrived at are, strictly speaking, without any justification in the text of the Qur'an. They can be legitimized only by alleged statements by the Prophet which we have no reason to regard as genuine.' As Reuben Levy writes in *The Social Structure of Islam* ([being the 2nd edn of *The*

Sociology of Islam], Cambridge University Press, 1965), the history of economic behaviour in Muslim societies, including South Asia, is one of adaptation to local norms and needs and, where appropriate, active participation in international financial mechanisms. One common interpretation is that the ban on excess profit, what in Western terminology would be 'usury' or 'profiteering', applies only to essential goods such as rice and dates.

42

The persistence of authoritarian regimes in the Arab world can be explained by the continued interference of Western powers.

Since the constitution of the Middle Eastern state system after 1918, Western powers have intervened on many occasions to sustain their existing allies and client states, sometimes overtly and sometimes covertly. The monarchs of Jordan, Oman and Morocco were, on occasion, rescued by overt external military assistance. Covert action has been seen in Iran, Syria, Oman and Yemen. Yet the importance of this should not overstated: equally numerous have been those cases where the West could not save it allies (Egypt [1952], Iraq [1958], Libya [1969], Iran [1979]) or hold onto its colonial position (Palestine [1948], Algeria [1962], South Yemen [1967]).

43

'Don't blame Arafat.' (*Guardian* headline, August 2004)

Yasser Arafat was the leader of the Palestinian Liberation
Organisation from 1967 until his death in 2004. While
sustaining the cause of Palestinian independence and remaining
a hero to many in the Arab world, measured retrospective
analysis has also to record that he proved to be a disastrous
political and military strategist, leading his people into
catastrophic wars in Jordan (1970–1) and Lebanon (1975–
82), while at the same time building his organisational base
around cronyism, corruption, intimidation and manipulation
of popular feeling. Given to demagogic speeches, he neither
maintained the support of the Arab states nor found a way,
consistently, to find common ground with Israelis prepared
to accept a two-state solution. After his return to the West
Bank and Gaza from exile in 1994 he built a ramshackle,

factional, kleptocratic and oppressive state, a pale replica of the worst of Arab nationalism of the 1950s. He successfully antagonised many in the West and in Israel who supported the Palestinian case for a viable state, and increasingly drove his own population into the arms of Islamist militants such as Islamic Jihad and Hamas.

44

The Gulf Cooperation Council, a six-member grouping of states comprising Saudi Arabia, Kuwait, Bahrain, Qatar, the United Arab Emirates and Oman, was set up in 1981 to promote integration of the six countries.

The real reason was not to promote greater integration, which is a remote possibility given the deep suspicions these rulers have of each other, but to make it more difficult for Iraq, then the dominant Arab military power in the Gulf – with ambitions to form a union in which it would control the oil-producing monarchies – to achieve its goals. The organisation should have really been named 'The Keep Saddam Hussein Out of the Gulf Council'. Masked as this was in the 1980s when Iraq was preoccupied with its war against Iran (which ended in 1988), this concern became entirely evident when, in August 1990, Iraq suddenly occupied Kuwait and proclaimed it Iraqi territory – its 'nineteenth province', no less.

45

The US, through its ambassador in Baghdad, April Glaspie, encouraged Saddam Hussein to invade Kuwait in August 1990.

We have no official US text of what Ambassador Glaspie said to Saddam during their last, fateful meeting on 25 July 1990 before the invasion of Kuwait on 2 August, but the text released by Iraq has not been challenged by Western authorities – although, in regard to the ambassador's words, it reads like a re-translation from Arabic back into English. (See Micah Sifry and Christopher Cerf, eds, *The Gulf War Readers: History, Documents, Opinions*, New York: Random House 1991.) In this transcript Glaspie is quoted as saying: 'I have a direct instruction from the president to seek better relations with Iraq.' Later, she does not endorse an Iraqi occupation of Kuwait, but only puts on record what had been general American policy and would normally be that of any foreign state in regard to border disputes between two Arab states. She states: 'We have no opinion on the Arab-Arab conflicts, like your border disagreements with Kuwait. I was in the American embassy in Kuwait during the late '60s. The instruction we had during this period was that we should express no opinion on this issue and that the issues are not associated with America.' This supposed 'green light' is very different to the much more substantial 'light' given to Israel before its invasion of Lebanon in July 1982.

46

With the Taif Accord of 1989, peace returned to Lebanon.

The Lebanese 'peace' is in some respects a mirage. Lebanon has seen an end of internal violence since December 1990, but the country remains under military occupation, while violence between Hizbullah in the south and Israeli forces has continued – with the prospect of much more to come. Moreover, despite a great deal of civil reconstruction and renewal (mostly in the capital, Beirut), Lebanese society remains deeply divided along confessional lines, while the social problems due to the severe poverty of a significant portion of the population continue.

47

The states of the Middle East can be divided into those that are historically deep-rooted and, by implication, therefore legitimate, and those which are 'artificial' colonial creations and, by implication, illegitimate.

All states in the world, in the sense of political, coercive and administrative entities that rule delimited territories and peoples, are modern creations. Some can claim anterior cultural, geographical or nomenclature derivation, ranging from those with three millennia of continuous existence as identifiable entities (such as China, Persia, Egypt or Yemen) to those which are the product of modern and accidental territorial delimitation and state coagulation – often, but not always, by colonialism. This includes all of East Asia, Africa, the Americas, Australasia and most of the Middle East. Legitimacy, the 'right' of a state and its people to exist as a separate entity, has no relation to historical existence or claims, which are usually inflated.

48

The division of the Arab world into over twenty separate states, and in defiance of the strong Arab desire in much of the twentieth century for *wahda* ('unity') is a result of Western policies keeping the Arabs divided along the lines of the imperial policy of 'divide and rule'. Equally, Islamist writers have blamed the West for sundering the hitherto unified character of the Muslim *umma* ('nation').

The role of the West in partitioning the Arab world after World War I is indisputable, but even then the existence of separate states reflected as much as anything the rivalries between different Arab rulers and the reluctance of distinct regional populations to share statehood or power with other Arabs. Over the decades distinct Arab states emerged with their own interests, not least those with access to oil revenue, which precluded further fusion and made even limited cooperation difficult, and often transient. To these inter-elite differences were added differences of popular sentiment – evident, for example, in relations between Saudi Arabia and Yemen in the Peninsula or between Egypt and Syria, with the population of the latter overthrowing a United Arab Republic with Egypt in 1961. Here a comparative element may help, since a rather similar process took place in Latin America in the first decades of the nineteenth century after the Spanish withdrawal: broad aspirations, inspired by Simón Bolívar, for Latin American unity foundered on regional, elite and popular resistance, which ended up yielding, as in the Arab world, around twenty distinct states.

The more general claim that imperialism and colonialism divide in order to rule is, in broad terms, simplistic: the overall record of colonialism has been to merge and unite previously disparate entities, be this in sixteenth-century Ireland, nineteenth-century India and Sudan or twentieth-century Libya and Southern Arabia. The British supported the formation of the League of Arab States in 1945 and tried, in the event unsuccessfully, to create united federations first in Southern Arabia (1962–7) and then in the Gulf states (1968–71). As Sami Zubaida has pointed out in his talks, imperialism in fact tends to unite and rule. It is independent states such as India and Pakistan (later Pakistan and Bangladesh), as well as Ireland, Cyprus and, indeed, the USSR and Yugoslavia, that promote fragmentation.

49

Western policy in the Gulf is guided by the 'well-known' principle, variously attributed to Sir Winston Churchill, Sir Percy Sykes and others: 'Feed the Arabs, Starve the Persians.'

No one knows who said this, and whoever did, it is a wholly simplistic and inaccurate summary of Western policy in that region in the twentieth century. Moreover, and despite the claims of Arabs and Persians alike to the contrary, it has been Western – i.e. up to 1968 UK, and thereafter US – policy to get Iran and the Arab states to collaborate, form an effective security and political alliance and settle their differences and suspicions through negotiation. That this has not happened is not the fault of London, Paris, Moscow or Washington.

50

The politics of Central Asia, the Caspian and the Trans-Caucasus region since the collapse of the USSR can be understood as another chapter in the nineteenth-century 'Great Game', whereby great powers act through their rivalries in the region.

The relevance of the nineteenth-century long-distance rivalry between an expanding Russia and British India to the present is virtually nil, a good example of facile but bogus historical analogy. First, in the nineteenth century the issue of oil and hence of exploration rights, pipelines and investment in the Central Asian states was irrelevant.

Secondly, the states themselves were not significant actors as, with their established post-communist kleptocratic elites, they are now.

Thirdly, China, Turkey and Iran, although independent

states then as now, were not – as they certainly are today – significant actors on the scene. Other, not trivial, features of the contemporary scene that were to all intents and purposes absent in the nineteenth century are Islamic fundamentalism and the narcotics trade.

51

Of all the areas of the world, or alternatively of the Third World, the Middle East was the one that suffered most during the Cold War.

Most of the conflicts of the Middle East between 1945–91 were certainly incorporated into, and exacerbated by, the Cold War, e.g. the Arab-Israeli, Iran-Iraq, Saudi-Yemeni and Syrian-Turkish disputes; but the Cold War was not the *cause* of any of them. Moreover, compared to East Asia, Southern Africa or Central America, the level of casualties and broader socioeconomic destruction was lesser. The most costly and protracted Middle East conflict of this era, the Iran-Iraq war of 1980–8, had nothing to do with the Cold War, as cause or effect.

52

The USSR invaded Afghanistan in December 1979 as part of a strategic drive towards the warm-water ports of the Indian Ocean.

This is another myth arising from Cold War fantasy rather than fact. It was evident – to some at least, at the time, and has been confirmed by the ample supply of Soviet documents thereafter – that the USSR, far from having engineered the April 1978 communist seizure of power in Kabul, and plotting then to send in troops as part of some broader drive to the Indian Ocean and the oilfields of the Gulf, was reacting in a cautious and often confused way to the growing instability inside Afghanistan. The despatch of Soviet forces in December 1979 was a last-ditch attempt, after months of refusing Afghan requests for aid, to save the People's Democratic Party of Afghanistan (PDPA) regime.

Much speculation about Soviet policy in the 1970s and 1980s, as about Russian policy today, invokes the 'Testament of Peter the Great', in which Russia is exhorted to gain access to the waters of the Indian Ocean. This testament is, however, a fake.

53

The Islamist *mujahidin* defeated the Soviet forces in Afghanistan in the 1980s.

This was one of the major claims of the Reagan administration in regard to the weakening of the USSR in the 1980s, the prelude to its collapse. It is also, even more importantly, the central claim to legitimacy of Osama Bin Laden and al-Qa'ida – indeed, Afghanistan is said to be the only Muslim 'victory' in modern times, a marked contrast to the failure to liberate Palestine or prevent the occupation and partition of the Arab world after World War I. All this is overstated. The Soviet 'limited contingent' of 130,000 troops (at most a quarter of the level of US forces in Vietnam, 1965–73) was sent in December 1979 to prevent the overthrow of the communist PDPA, a regime first established in Kabul in 1978. This they did, until their negotiated withdrawal in 1988. Following their withdrawal, the PDPA regime survived, only falling in April 1992 after the withdrawal of Russian financial support. The campaign of the counter-revolutionary Islamic guerrillas, and the later ending of Moscow's material aid to Kabul, were organised by Western, Saudi and Pakistani intelligence services – without whom the Afghan *mujahidin* would have been confined to the mountains.

54

The underlying reason for the emergence of chaos and Islamist violence in Afghanistan in the 1990s was that the West had, after forcing the Russians to leave in 1989, abandoned interest in or activities related to that country.

Nothing could be further from the truth: far from 'forgetting' or 'abandoning' Afghanistan, the West, in violation of the April 1988 UN agreement on a Soviet withdrawal, continued to arm and finance the rebels and in the end brought down the reforming communist regime. In April 1988 the 'West', i.e. the US, Britain and its allies, Egypt and Pakistan, signed an agreement to stop supplying the Islamist guerrillas in Afghanistan in return for a withdrawal of Soviet forces. The Soviets left by February 1989, but aid to the guerrillas continued with the intention of forcing a collapse of the communist regime in Kabul. The US at the same time pressed hard for a cutoff in Soviet support for the Afghan regime after their troop withdrawal, but this was not successful until the change of government in Moscow following the failed coup of August 1991; then, in a deal brokered by US Secretary of State James Baker, Moscow cut off all aid to its former ally in Kabul. The regime of President Najibullah, who had held power since 1987, fell the following April.

55

During the 1970s Soviet policy in the Middle East in general, and in the Persian Gulf in particular, could be explained by a growing concern in Moscow about its declining oil output and its plans to seize Gulf oil to meet its own needs.

This was one of the more enduring and baseless Western myths about the Soviet Union in the 1970s. If the USSR had a plan to seize Gulf oil, this would have been as part of pre-empting of Western access to that oil, on which the latter most certainly was dependent, rather than to meet its own needs. During the 1970s Soviet oil output remained around 12 million barrels a day, the largest in the world, of which around 4 million barrels a day were exported. The connection between Gulf oil and the USSR that did matter was that Moscow, although not a member of the Organisation of Petroleum Exporting Countries (OPEC) cartel, was a free rider, in effect a beneficiary of the latter's increases in oil prices in 1973–4; some economists argue, indeed, that this unexpected boom in revenue prolonged the life of the now 'stagnant' Soviet system (as it came to be called) longer than would otherwise have been the case. So, far from there being an oil crisis in 1970s Russia, there was if anything, and in no way as a result of any Soviet policy initiative, an oil bonanza.

56

During the Cold War, the Palestinian resistance movement, and in particular Arafat's al-Fatah, were instruments of Soviet influence in the Middle East and followed Soviet instructions.

Relations between the USSR and the PLO were never easy. Moscow had, in the first place, recognised Israel in 1948, even before Washington, and had initially perceived Arab nationalism as being reactionary, 'feudal' and pro-British forces in the region. When the PLO emerged in the 1960s, the Soviets were reluctant to support or recognise it; when Arafat made his first visit to Moscow, in a plane bringing President Nasser on an official visit, he had to hide in the plane until the welcome ceremonies were over so that he would not be seen. In the 1970s and 1980s more formal relations developed, but there was never trust or agreement between the two sides. In particular, the USSR always insisted that the basis for any settlement of the Arab-Israeli dispute was the recognition of separate Israeli and Palestinian states, something the PLO refused to accept until 1988.

The claim that PLO finances came from Moscow was frequently heard after the end of the Cold War, in Israel in particular and among pro-Israelis in Europe and the US. The exact details of the PLO's finances are not and may never be known, but there is enough evidence to paint the broad picture: support from Arab states, particularly Gulf countries, in the late 1960s and early 1970s, then the levying of taxes and protection-racket income from Lebanon in the late 1960s and after, beyond which the PLO became manager – through myriad outlets and hidden investments – of a fund reckoned by some to be up to US$50 billion. This privatisation of the funds of guerrilla organisations was most extreme in the case of the PLO, but was evident elsewhere in the 1980s and 1990s (in Latin America, Africa and Asia above all) as a result of the availability in these areas of income from drugs and other illegally traded sources like diamonds.

57

The Iranian Revolution was not a rising up of the Iranian people but was initiated by, alternatively, the KGB; the BBC; Afghans bussed in by the *mullahs*; a petit-bourgeois faction of urban traders (*bazaaris*).

There is considerable political and sociological literature on the Iranian Revolution of 1978–9, relating it to broader theories of political and social change, but we still lack a sound historical narrative and empirical account of the events themselves using the documentary material and interviews that exist of this major historical event. The causes of the revolution were much disputed at the time and have remained controversial ever since. Side by side with the myths of Cold War, claiming a Soviet role and advantage when there was nothing of either, have come the myths originating with various strands of Iranian nationalists, monarchists and liberals that deny the central organisational and ideological role of the *mullahs*. No definitive refutation of these misleading accounts can be made, but more grounded and plausible explanations can be provided.

58

The Shah of Iran was overthrown in 1978–9 because of a shift in American policy, whereby the US decided to remove him – or, in the words of his autobiography, *The Shah's Story*, to throw him out 'like a dead mouse'.

Ultimately this myth rests on the fallacy that underlies much more radical anti-US thinking – namely that the US is all-powerful and therefore that anything that happens in any country must be the result of US policy. The reality is that, by the last months of 1978, and only three years after the ignominious US flight from Vietnam, the popular mobilisation against the Shah was so strong that there was nothing the US could do to maintain him.

59

Israel received decisive help from the US in launching the 1967 Arab-Israeli war, which was part of a broader offensive at that time against socialist and pro-Soviet allies (Indonesia and Ghana [1965], Algeria [1966] and Greece [1967]).

There is little evidence that these disparate events, beyond their being perceived as somehow connected, had a common cause. This was, in any case, a moment when the global conjuncture appeared to be moving against the US, as the war in South Vietnam escalated, forcing Washington to send over half a million troops to Indochina. The outbreak of the 1967 Arab-Israeli war was not a result of some global strategy, but of a set of specific, regional calculations and miscalculations; on one hand, Israel's long-standing wish to strike at the growing military power of Egypt and, on the other, the tactical mistakes of Nasser in May of that year, through which he requested the withdrawal of UN buffer forces and so left himself open to the Israeli attack.

60

Egypt launched the 1973 Arab-Israeli war at the instigation of the USSR, this being part of a broader Soviet offensive then underway in the Third World, leading to the revolution in Ethiopia (1974); the communist victories in Vietnam, Laos and Cambodia (1975); the Movimento Popular de Libertação de Angola's drive for power in that country (1975); the revolutions in Afghanistan (1978) and Iran (1979); and the revolutionary seizures of power in Grenada and Nicaragua (March and July 1979 respectively), as well as, among other things, the rise of 'state-sponsored terrorism' in the Middle East and beyond.

This is the standard generalised indictment of Soviet 'misconduct' in the Third World that underlay the collapse of *détente* in the mid- and late 1970s, the rise of Ronald Reagan in the US and the onset of what I and some others have termed 'the Second Cold War'. Much of this was exaggeration and false, conspiratorial analysis of separate regional and local developments which had little to do with each other, except in their cumulative rejection of Western hegemony, and often had nothing to do with the policy or influence of the USSR, overt or covert. The Egyptian attack on Israel in 1973 reflected the political calculations of President Anwar Sadat – the aim of which was to do a deal with Israel and the US and in the process expel the USSR from its bases in Egypt and undo its influence there. (This is, in the end, what occurred.) I have gone into this period in greater detail in *The Making of the Second Cold War* (Verso Books, London, 1983).

61

In the 1970s, the Arab world acquired an 'Oil Weapon' which it used to effect on the international stage, in particular to win support for Palestine.

The 'Oil Weapon' was never effective. Financial power is, in itself, rarely a sufficient basis for influencing the policies of other states, as Arab producers found with regard to other Arab countries in the 1970s and again during the Kuwait crisis of 1990–1; in relations with the industrialised and militarily more powerful world of the Organisation for Economic Cooperation and Development (OECD), this was even more so. The threat to 'use' the 'Oil Weapon' caused considerable alarm in the West in the early 1970s, and there was certainly a possibility of financial instability and temporary oil shortages. Hence the establishment of the International Energy Agency (IEA). But, divorced from any effective military power and with there being nowhere else but the OECD to whom to sell oil to – or with financial and other markets in which to invest – the threats proved empty. Some subsequent attempts to revive this 'weapon', e.g. by Saddam Hussein in the 1990s, fizzled out. More than thirty years after the 1973 brandishing of the 'Oil Weapon', the Arab oil states remain almost wholly dependent on oil for their foreign exchange and state revenues and their societies are even less adjusted to the world economy in terms of administrative and educational levels than was the case in the 1970s. Whether or not theories of non-military of 'soft' power (as developed by Joseph Nye of Harvard) apply even to the US, they certainly do not describe the reality of the Middle East.

62

During the war in Yemen, in which it participated with up to 70,000 troops from 1962–7, Egypt emerged the loser. Yemen was, in effect, Egypt's 'Vietnam'.

Egypt sent troops to Yemen in 1962 after revolutionary officers overthrew the imamate, or monarchy, and proclaimed a republic. The new state was challenged by royalists, supporters of the old regime, and backed by Saudi Arabia and Britain, and for the next five years the Egyptian forces defended the republic in a bitter war. The Egyptian forces withdrew in October 1967, after Egypt's defeat in the June war with Israel, but despite royalist attempts to capture the Yemeni capital, Sanaa, the republic survived. In 1970 a peace agreement was signed, under which most royalists returned to the country and were integrated into the new political and economic system. The republic had been successfully defended. This was not, despite claims to this effect – some of them from Egyptians themselves – the equivalent of the US war in Vietnam or the Russian war in Afghanistan. Yemen was, in the years prior to World War I, the 'Vietnam' of the Ottoman Empire, but not that of Egypt. In Yemen, Egypt attained its political goals. The republic survived.

63

The military represents, or at least in the 1950s and 1960s represented, a 'modernising elite' – alternatively, the 'new men' – in the Middle East.

The seizure of power by armies in the Middle East, as throughout Europe and in Japan in the interwar period (1918–39), reflected not some advance for modernity or 'national' forces but the control of the state by a rival elite. These elites, to be sure, used some modernising language and methods, but did so the better to control the population and fend off external pressures, and to legitimate their own corporate and collective appropriation of economic assets through state positions and salaries, and through direct administration of now-nationalised assets for their own purposes. The economic trading organisations characteristic of many Middle Eastern military regimes exemplifies this (Egypt, pre-2003 Iraq, Syria, Yemen).

64

The revolutions and nationalist military revolts that ended the monarchies of so many Middle Eastern states 'liberated' their people from political oppression and tyranny.

This was a comforting myth of the 1950s and beyond. These events certainly broke the power of the old regimes and, for a time, brought the populations of their countries into active political and social life. But by any broad human rights criteria, the republican regimes of the region were responsible for far more killing, brutality, oppression and, often, corruption and theft of the people's wealth than were the monarchies. Between, on the one side the Shah of Iran, Nuri Said of Iraq and King Faruq of Egypt and, on the other, the Islamic Republic, the Iraqi Ba'th Party and the militaristic junta that has ruled Egypt since 1952, there is no comparison. As with everywhere in the modern world, revolutions strengthened, not weakened states, and 'liberation' came at a price.

65

The organisation that ruled Iraq until the American invasion in March 2003, the Arab Ba'th Socialist Party, was a radical anti-imperialist party.

The ideology of the Ba'th was a mixture of fascist, romantic and communist elements, and its relations with the West were equally mixed. In the late 1950s and early 1960s, leading up to its first coup in March 1963, the Ba'th in general, and Saddam Hussein in particular, had relations with the US intelligence services. On the testimony of King Hussein of Jordan, we learn that the CIA collaborated actively with the Ba'th in its coup of March 1963, which led to the killing of thousands of communist opponents. Later, in the 1980s, the US and other Western countries actively supported Iraq in the war against Iran, which Iraq itself had launched. Among many distinguished visitors to Baghdad during this period was, on two occasions, later-US Defense Secretary Donald Rumsfeld, as an envoy of then-President Reagan.

66

The Middle East never exhibited a strong affinity for communism, because of the atheistic nature of Marxist ideology.

From the 1920s onwards, and even more so under the impact of World War II in the 1940s, the Middle East had a strong communist presence in several countries. The first Communist Party to be founded in the whole of Asia was that of Iran in June 1920, and in the late 1940s and early 1950s the Tudeh ('Masses') Party had the support of around 25 per cent of the population. It was, indeed, the only real party in modern Iranian history since then. In a number of Arab countries – Iraq, Egypt, Sudan, Lebanon – the Communist Party was also a significant political factor. In Palestine, the only organisation to sustain the campaign for Palestinian rights in the 1960s and 1970s in Israel proper was the Communist Party. In two Middle Eastern states, the People's Democratic Republic of

Yemen and the Democratic Republic of Afghanistan, what were in effect communist parties – though they affected other names (The Yemeni Socialist Party, The People's Democratic Party of Afghanistan) – were in power for substantial periods of time (1967–94 and 1978–92, respectively).

The claim that Arab and Islamic cultures or national aspirations and communism were incompatible was a standard counter-revolutionary theme of monarchs, *ulema* and Western statesmen alike in the Cold War period. The ultimate irony of the influence of communism was that those who opposed it so ferociously – first the Ba'th Party and then the Islamists – borrowed heavily from its ideological framework and organisational model. (For the influence of Marxism on the ideology of Ayatollah Khomeini, see Ervand Abrahamian, *Khomeinism*, London, I. B. Tauris, 1993.) Khomeini, beyond his denunciations of 'world-devouring' *jahankhor* imperialism, also celebrated 1 May as the Festival of the Islamic Worker. He cited a *hadith* (a saying of the Prophet) to the effect that the sweat of the worker meant more in the eyes of Allah than the prayers of the faithful.

In Sudan, the National Islamic Front, which came to power in 1989 with a programme of radical Sunni Islamism at home and abroad, had for more than three decades modelled itself on the ideas and organisational practices, as well as the utopian internationalism, of communism.

67

Zionism, i.e. the project of creating a Jewish state in the Middle East, was a product of a broader Western campaign to divide and subjugate the Arab and Muslim worlds.

This frequently-made claim assumes a much closer relation between the Zionist movement, established in 1897 at a conference in Basle, Switzerland, and the major states of the time. The origins of Zionism lie in political and intellectual discussion in Europe in the latter part of the nineteenth century amongst Jews concerned about the rise of anti-Semitism, especially in the Czarist Russian empire but also in Western Europe. As such Zionism was a spontaneous, in contemporary terms 'non-governmental' movement which, as any such movement or NGO (non-governmental organisation) does, sought to win governments over to its side. None of the major powers either created, funded or consistently supported the goal of a Jewish state until World War II when, in the face of Nazi persecution of European Jews, the US, the USSR and later Britain came to accept this goal. The assimilation of Zionism as a non-state social and political movement with imperial strategy in the Middle East in the first part of the twentieth century is, therefore, a simplification.

68

Palestinian nationalism is a creation of Arab states and manipulated by them to put pressure on Israel.

This is to some degree a reverse version of the preceding myth about Zionism. The Arab states certainly played a role in the diplomacy of the Palestine question before Israel was created in 1948; they then went to war with Israel in May of that year, and have sought subsequently if ineffectually to promote a Palestinian cause. Moreover, the first sign of a re-emerging Palestinian political identity, the creation of the Palestine Liberation Organisation in 1964, was the result of an Arab League of States initiative. But this manoeuvring and frequent posturing by Arab states was separate from the attempts by Palestinian representatives themselves, from the 1920s onwards, to promote their own cause. Even in the darkest times of the 1950s and early 1960s, autonomous

Palestinian groups and nationalists – who later emerged as al-Fatah on one hand and the more radical Popular and Democratic Fronts on the other – were independent of the Arab states' control. Within occupied Palestine the Communist Party continued to articulate Palestinian ideas. After the war of 1967 the Palestinian organisations all sought to build alliances with the states of the region and beyond; however, it was not the Arab states' but Israel's refusal to allow a viable Palestinian state to emerge that shaped the content and tone of Palestinian nationalism.

69

Israel was established as a 'Light unto the Nations'.

The term 'Light unto the Nations' is a Biblical term intended to convey a particular moral character, and religious legitimacy to the Jewish state established after 1948. Analogous to claims of some special sanctified superiority claimed by, among others, the Americans, the British and the Russians at different times in modern history, it served to seriously distort the character of this state. Far from being especially moral or exemplary, Israel acquired a political and economic system that was rife with clientelism, venality and patronage, all accentuated by the inherently unstable nature of the proportional representation system it adopted. It was, in comparative terms, just another corrupt southern Mediterranean country.

In the international domain, Israel became a garrison state, reliant on armed force to preserve itself and, after 1967, to hold down and brutalise the Palestinians under its control, all of this accompanied by a cacophony of accusation and defamation of those who criticised its policies and values, gentile and Jew alike. Herzl's original vision in his 1896 book *Der Judenstaat* ('The State of the Jews'), that the soldier would stay in the barracks just as the rabbi would stay in the temple, proved cruelly mistaken for Jews and Arabs alike. The degree of military influence in the society was evident not only in the enormous proportion of state finances consumed by the armed forces but also in the prominence within the political system of those with military backgrounds: in the first fifty-six years of its existence, i.e. up to 2004, Israel had nine prime ministers. Of these one was a conventional military figure (Yitzhak Rabin), while no less than four others had, on available evidence, been associated with acts of illegality and contraventions of the rules of war, i.e. terrorism (Menachem Begin, Yitzhak Shamir, Ehud Barak and Ariel Sharon).

At the same time, the pseudo-sacred nature of the term 'Light unto the Nations' concealed the very remarkable, if short-lived, secular achievement of early Israeli society in creating among Jews a society that reached perhaps further than any other non-coercive modern experiment in egalitarian, experimental living, epitomised by the *kibbutz* system. This experiment, born out of the socialist ideals of some of the early Zionists, involved far-reaching measures to allow communal living; a reduction (when not abolition) of gender differences; and shared parenting and collective ownership. It was also a robust secular commitment to shaking off the clerical and Hasidic shackles of the Eastern European Jewish tradition. It was not to survive the changes in Israeli society of the 1960s and 1970s and has, undeservedly, been almost ignored in later discussions of twentieth-century socialist living and experimentation.

70

Israel is not a colonial or settler state.

The claim, promoted by Zionism, that Israel is *not* a colonial state rests on two premises: one, that Israel is a recreation of an ancient and divinely sanctioned state, and that this gives it both legitimacy and a historical, primordial character independent of European, colonialism of the modern period; secondly, that to admit the colonial character of Israel is to deny its legitimacy as a state, since colonialism lacks legal or moral authority. Both of these arguments bear re-examination. The first involves the relevance, ethical or legal, of ancient and religiously sanctioned claims. There is little point in equivocating on this: such claims have, in contemporary international law, zero validity, however strongly they are articulated or supposedly 'felt' (i.e. after massive efforts have gone into educational, political and nationalist incitement).

The second argument needs disentangling, as so often, through comparison. If by 'colonial' is meant not acting directly on behalf of colonial powers – which few if any states do or did, and Zionism certainly did not – but rather having come into existence in the context of, with some assistance from and with many of the values of the European imperial and colonial project, then Israel most certainly is a colonial state. It was created on the basis of European values of cultural superiority and the right to occupy the lands of others as a means of solving a particularly European problem, that of anti-Semitism, and with the support and – when not support, connivance – of European and North American states. It necessarily, not contingently, involved the displacement, destruction and subjugation of another people and land. This was the argument made, in cogent and learned form, by the French Marxist writer Maxime Rodinson in the 1960s, and it has not been overtaken by subsequent analysis or writing.

Israel is but one of dozens of contemporary states, the general legitimacy of which is not contested, that came into existence in this way, i.e. all the countries of the Americas, most of Africa, Australia and, of course, with the exception of Iran, Saudi Arabia and Turkey, all the states of the Middle East. States and nations were created which, in the rather short space of two or so generations, became functioning societies. Israel is, in this sense, neither more nor less legitimate than dozens of other states in the world; but the claim to statehood and recognition rests not on some particularity of history, religion or internal conduct, but on this shared and necessary feature of the modern world.

71

The 1917 Balfour Declaration on the part of the said-named British foreign secretary was promoted by British Jews seeking to win support for the goal of the Zionist movement, the establishment of a Jewish state – carefully phrased as a 'Jewish Home' – in Palestine.

In fact, and contrary to much later arguments to the above effect by supporters and opponents of Zionism alike, many of the main representatives of the British Jewish community were opposed to this policy, seeing it as a means of promoting the departure of Jews from Britain. Edwin Samuel Montagu, the one Jewish member of the British cabinet at the time, opposed it, on the grounds that it could promote hostility in the Middle East.

72

The Zionist movement, founded in 1897, did not originally intend to create a Jewish state in Palestine, just a 'homeland' or community.

This is a pervasive and no doubt necessary fiction that Zionist leaders maintained in the period before 1948 in order to lessen opposition to them. Thus Zionist policy was often publicly phrased in terms that seemed to deny the goal of a Jewish state and to cast the decision to go for such a state as a result of British and/or Arab intolerance. In reality, the aim of Zionism was always that of a fully separate and independent state. It could not have been otherwise, given that this was the standard, modular, goal of all nationalist movements in the twentieth century. Theodor Herzl, speaking of the founding conference of 1897, was clear; in his *Journals*, he wrote: 'At Basle, I created the Jewish state. If I said that publicly today, it would be met by general laughter. Perhaps in five years, certainly in fifty, everyone will understand.' He was nine months off.

73

The nationalist movements that emerged in the Iranian provinces of Azerbaijan and Kurdistan in the 1940s, and which were crushed when these areas were re-occupied by Iranian forces in December 1946, were separatist, i.e. aiming to detach these regions from Iran itself.

The claim of 'separatism' is often used in Iranian, and indeed Middle Eastern, politics to discredit political forces that aspire to a greater and, on democratic grounds quite legitimate, degree of political and cultural autonomy. In Arabic the term *infisali* ('separatist'), is a particular term of abuse, harking back to the breakaway by Syria in 1961 from the United Arab Republic, created with Gamal Abdel Nasser's Egypt in 1958. In the case of Iran, the movements in Azerbaijan and Kurdistan did not proclaim independence, or aspire in their statements and programmes to it. Rather, their political leaderships called for greater autonomy from Tehran and a recognition of the linguistic and cultural rights of the Azeri and Kurdish peoples respectively. They took advantage of the presence in both areas of Soviet forces – who had entered Iran in alliance with Britain in 1941 as part of their overall World War II strategy – to assert ethnic and regional rights. The claim that they were 'separatist' was used by the Shah's army to destroy all autonomy in these regions and became part of the mythology of the Cold War in the region.

After the fall of the Shah in January 1979, the same story was to repeat itself with, this time, the Islamist authorities in Tehran accusing the Azeri and Kurdish secular democrats who wanted federal rights of secession.

74

The history of World War I and its aftermath in the Middle East demands understanding the importance of the British official T. E. Lawrence, often known as 'Lawrence of Arabia'.

T. E. Lawrence was a minor, when not marginal, figure in the modern history of the Middle East, whose importance has been subsequently blown out of all proportion. This is partly a result of a newspaper campaign romanticising him in the 1920s and partly a result of a British concern to conceal London's betrayal of Arab nationalism by highlighting the activities of someone sympathetic to the 'Arab' cause (as if there were only one), but also, in the Middle Eastern context, a means by which those who lost out in the battle for control of Arabia and the Hijaz in the 1920s (the Hashemites, with whom Lawrence worked) can magnify their own role in these events. The reality indicates a much more reduced role. Lawrence himself was not a military but just a political officer, attached to the irregular Arab forces provided by the then-Hashemite ruler of Hijaz, Sharif Hussein. Hussein's forces comprised 3,000 untrained and irregular troops, compared to the 250,000 British and Indian regular soldiers who conducted the campaign against the Ottomans. Lawrence's book *The Seven Pillars of Wisdom* is a fine piece of prose, but as a source for studying the history or society of the Arab world it is almost worthless. Lawrence's qualifications for analysing the region must also be cast in question by the fact that, for all the mystique about his understanding of 'the Arab', his competence in the language was very limited.

75

The West has, since at the latest the early nineteenth century and more particularly since World War I and the subsequent Treaty of Sèvres (1920), been deeply hostile to the independence, integrity and stability of Turkey. It has sought by a number of means, including exploiting the Cyprus, Armenian and, more recently, Kurdish issues to undermine Turkish aspirations.

The Turkish suspicion of 'Western' policy (as ever, seen as both something common to all European and North American states, and as timelessly constant from 1920, or indeed 1620) is a simplification. Prior to World War II, European states were as likely to ally with the Ottomans as to oppose them. The immediate cause of the collapse of the Ottoman Empire was the decision, taken by the Turkish leaders themselves, to join World War I on the side of other European powers, Germany and Austria. The policy of Western states regarding

Turkey since then, and including before and after World War II, has been varied and flexible, reflecting not a deep agenda but interest and calculation. On the Kurdish question, about which most Turks have been so concerned, the 'West' has – some statements of solidarity and anguish apart – done virtually nothing to oppose Turkish interests.

76

The Islamic world has a model for a political system in the form of government founded by the Prophet Muhammad in 630 AD and carried forward by his four immediate successors, or *caliphs.*

The early decades of Islam are hardly a very encouraging model, even assuming it was applicable to the world of fourteen centuries later. Of the four *caliphs*, the first, Abu Bakr, lived less than two years – too short a time to validate any political system – and the other three, Umar, Uthman and Ali, were all murdered.

77

Contemporary political and social developments can only be understood by reference to ancient, centuries-old – if not millennia-old – conflicts: the Medes and the Persians; the sons of Abraham; the desert ('brown') and the fertile ('green'); the sons of Adnan and of Qahtan; Sunnis and Shi'is; the followers of Yezid or Mu'awiya versus those of Hussein and Ali ... to name but a few.

All history before the living memory of those currently involved in politics must be tested as an explanatory framework to analyse the present. There are causes and factors that go back before the recent past, but the onus of proof is on those who assert such long-term causation, not on those often-beleaguered modernists who doubt this trans-epochal continuity. If identities and animosities of centuries or more are used to explain and/or justify current behaviour and events, this can only be explained by referring to the mechanisms of socialisation to which societies and authorities resort – often with various forms of violence – not as natural outcomes of some inherent but ethereal social continuity. The resort to explanation in terms of ancient heroes, wars, hatreds is an escape from explanation rather than a contribution to it.

78

The peoples, and states, of the region have been more or less at war for hundreds, perhaps thousands, of years.

There have been many wars in the Middle East, in the distant and more recent past. There may well be more. But in modern times the Middle East has been no more riven by war than other parts of the world such as Africa and East Asia, and, in the past century, much less than its neighbouring continent to the northeast, Europe. For all the wars between the Ottomans and Safavis (later Qajars), the two empires coexisted reasonably well for four centuries (1500–1914). In the period since 1945 there have been five Arab-Israeli wars but these, while catastrophic for the Palestinians, have been confined in time and space. Only the Iran-Iraq war of 1980–8 escaped external and regional state control and involved, by modern standards, high levels of casualties.

79

The religions of the Middle East – notably Islam, Christianity, Judaism – are, if their holy texts are consulted, 'religions of peace'.

The whole argument about religious texts as being for or against a particular form of action, be it war, capitalism, environmental protection or the equality of men and women, is mistaken. Religious texts, beyond certain core items relating to belief, contain variant prescriptions and judgements about social and political life including armed hostility between groups and states. For those who want to use them, there are passages that condone, when not encouraging, violent acts towards people who are not members of the group in question, and which can be and have, in modern times, been used to justify terrible atrocities. The choice is not given by the religion or text; the authority for 'peace' in the Middle East is not given by religion, nor by the men authorised to represent and interpret it, but is a result of explicit and contemporary decisions.

80

Alternatively, the religions of the Middle East are 'religions of war'.

This is the obverse simplification to that found in the preceding myth. The same argument applies: there are plenty of bases in the holy texts, histories and traditions of Middle Eastern religions on which to construct a modern politics and international law of cooperation, respect for the general rules of war and coexistence between states and communities. Moreover, while it is possible – as is often the case – to use religious authority to legitimise modern nationalism and the claims of specific nationalisms (Zionist, Iranian, pan-Arab, local Arab), there is also in each religion a strong element of universalism and appeals for a shared humanity within a recognition of the positive diversity of peoples, cultures *and* religions.

81

The behaviour of Middle Eastern states and peoples can be explained by reference to the prescriptions of a set of holy texts.

Religion, beyond symbols and the occasional but ineffective gesture of solidarity, does not provide any guide to explaining or assessing the foreign policies of regional states. When it comes to arms races, oil prices, controlling migration, the pressures of globalisation and much else besides, religion is irrelevant, except as an idiom. Where there are supposed conflicts between the authority of a religious text or tradition and the pressures of modern politics, e.g. on sovereignty, human rights, the environment or the claims of nationalism, religion has proven to be adaptable, once those with power so wish.

82

Ancient texts, supposedly given by 'God', legitimate current political and social aspirations to power and contemporary, in effect nationalist, territorial claims.

In contemporary politics and society, legitimacy derives or should derive from legal and constitutional principles, and from international law and norms. In such contexts, and in regard to disputes that arise within them, the claims of the supernatural, the divine, the 'traditional' have no standing. Where they are invoked this is as a function of contemporary nationalist instrumentalisation of the past, particularly as far as claims to territory are concerned. All such claims, and all assertions of feeling, 'hurt', affection and the like with regard to territory should be discounted.

83

The peoples involved in the Arab-Israeli dispute are in conflict over holy land, on the basis of claims derived from holy texts.

As earth, rocks, trees and rivers have no religious character, there cannot, as such, be such a thing as a 'holy' land. If land is valued, in human terms, it is because people live, love, work and die on it, without claims to special divine or other interventions, or other exclusionary aspirations. Nor are there any such thing as 'holy' texts. The written word is put there by human beings; by, in large measure if not entirely, men. Any reasonable, textually educated specialist who examines the 'holy' texts of Middle Eastern religions would see at once that these texts are composites, written at different times by different hands and in different circumstances. Hence their flexibility and, at times, their charm.

84

The city of Jerusalem has for centuries been an object of reverence and longing on the part of Christians, Jews and Muslims. Contemporary Jerusalem 'is' or alternatively 'should be', by some divine ordinance wholly Jewish, or Muslim, or Arab, or something.

Christians have made much of Jerusalem as the site of the crucifixion of Jesus Christ, but other centres of political and religious power – notably Rome and Byzantium (but also, for Orthodox Christians, Kiev and, for Armenians, St Echmiatsin) – have historically been more important. The sacking of Jerusalem by the Crusaders in 1099 and the massacre of its Muslim and Jewish inhabitants showed little respect for that city, and it was a dispute over the keys to the Church of the Holy Sepulchre which sparked the Crimean War in 1854.

As for Jews and Muslims, the obsession with Jerusalem

has been much talked up by nationalists in recent decades. While Jews had a religious devotion to 'Zion' (see Glossary), this was a spiritual as much as broader religious commitment. It is noticeable that during the centuries of the Ottoman Empire, when Jews settled in many Middle Eastern cities, few went to live in Jerusalem. For Muslims the city is the site of the al-Aqsa mosque, said to be the scene of the *miraj* ('Night Journey') of the Prophet Muhammad, but for most of the fourteen centuries of Islamic history Jerusalem was a provincial town. In the time of the Ottoman Empire, it was not even the capital of a separate province, or *vilayet*. In the early years of the Zionist movement, when secularist pragmatism prevailed, Jewish leaders such as David Ben-Gurion did not make control of a united Jerusalem a priority. The talking up of an 'indivisible' Jerusalem by Jewish and Arab politicians dates in large measure from the 1967 Arab-Israeli war.

Religious and supposedly divinely ordained claims to Jerusalem refer, inasmuch as they have any validity at all, to a tiny proportion of the existing municipal area of Jerusalem – this latter drawn up by Israeli officials after 1967. The historical city to which claims hark back is one square mile of walled area. In some ways, the truth about Jerusalem was given unwittingly after 2003 by Kurdish nationalists who claimed that the city of Kirkuk, disputed between Kurds and Arabs, was 'the Kurdish Jerusalem'. If this was meant to imply that Kirkuk had some historic, sacred, character it was wholly false, but if it was meant to mean that it had become, because of modern nationalism and contemporary migration, a site of inter-ethnic conflict, it was accurate – but as a comment on Jerusalem rather than on Kirkuk. The conclusion is that far from Kirkuk being the Kurdish Jerusalem, Jerusalem had become the Jewish and Arab Kirkuk, i.e. an overblown, chauvinist fetish, and the object of arbitrarily intransigent nationalist demands on both sides. It would be reasonable to assume that this is a conclusion with which *no one* in the region, be they Jew, Arab or Kurd, would concur. This does not make it the less valid.

85

Legal texts justified as divinely sanctioned – Jewish *halakhah*, Islamic *shari'ah*, Christian canon law – can provide a workable and clear foundation for legal systems in the modern world.

Traditionally there was some analogy, but also considerable difference, between the scope and claims made for religious law in the three main religions. The most developed legal system was the *halakhah* and the least, the *shari'ah*, with Christian canon law somewhere in the middle. Even in the case of *halakhah* there was no single, divinely sanctioned legal code, but rather a legal system built up, with varying schools of interpretation, on the basis of some legally relevant elements in the holy texts. *Shari'ah* in the sense of legal principles in the Qur'an itself is very scant, with about eighty of the 6,000 verses of the Qur'an being concerned with legal questions, and most of these concerning personal relations. What did develop in Islam was *fiqh*, or jurisprudence, the body of law accumulated over centuries through legal cases, and itself divided into different schools, four Sunni, and Shi'i. A person competent in *fiqh* is a *faqih* – generally a term of respect, but in modern Arabic usage also a term for (in politics but also love) a person out of touch with reality, a 'dreamer'.

86

The problem with Islam is that it is in need of a 'Reformation'.

This injunction, repeated by some Muslim reformers as well as Western observers, confuses several issues. First of all, if by 'Reformation' is meant a period of debate, rational discussion of religion and the rejection of a single religious authority such as the Vatican, then Islam has long exhibited such tendencies. Islam, without a Vatican, has no concept of heresy. There never was, after 661 AD and the division between Sunni and Shi'i, a single authority, and there is not even a formal religious hierarchy as in Christianity.

If by 'Reformation' is meant religious thinking freed of dogmatism, then the history of Islamic thought has long been characterised by rationalist and open trends, notably that of the Mu'tazilis (eighth and ninth centuries AD), who criticised dogmatic thinking and were supported by Caliph al-Mamun in 827 AD and the Andalusian philosopher Ibn 'Arabi (died 1273). For centuries Muslim thinkers, largely but not only Shi'is, have practised what is termed *ijtihad*, independent and critical interpretation of sacred texts and traditions. More recently, in the twentieth century, there have been many Muslim thinkers who have reviewed, in an open and critical spirit, the claims and interpretation of Islam.

However, this call for a 'Reformation' also misrepresents other issues. On one hand it ascribes to the Protestantism that followed the Reformation a freedom of spirit and a tolerance of secular debate that is markedly absent from much of today's Protestantism, as is evident in the fervent intolerance of the US. On the other hand, and most importantly, it confuses cause and effect: Arab society and much of the Muslim world are not dictatorial, authoritarian or intellectually paralysed because of religion, but the other way around – it is the existence, for other reasons, of such states and societies that itself produces a paralysed religion. The solution to censorship in the Arab world, for example, or the inequality of women, is not to be found in changing religious doctrine or interpretation, but in changing society and the state themselves. For its part, Islam is capable of greater theological flexibility, starting from the principle – which is available for use by those who so choose – that the verses of the Qur'an, instead of being one block of unchallengeable dogma, divide into those which are *nasikh* (i.e. which prevail), and those which are *mansukh* (i.e. prevailed over). To most Muslims, for example, verses on stoning criminals to death or on slavery are, in the contemporary world, *mansukh*.

87

Muslims of the Middle East have, for religious reasons, a particular resistance to rule by or substantive interaction with non-Muslims.

This is one of the most ridiculous generalisations of modern politics. The resistance by Muslims to rule by non-Muslims is not a function of religion at all, but of the rise of the dominant Western secular ideology of modern times, nationalism, with its core ideological claim that peoples are entitled to sovereignty and independence on a given, 'national' area of territory. Prior to the rise of nationalisms, Muslims lived without major revolt under non-Muslim rulers – most evidently, in the British and Czarist Russian empires. Isolation from the outside world and a recurrent xenophobia have marked many Islamic states, as they have non-Muslim counterparts from mediaeval China to modern fascist and communist regimes, but the overall history of the Muslim world has been one of interaction through trade and cultural exchange with the non-Muslim world: east to India, south to Africa and west and northwards to Europe.

88

Islam is a religion of the desert.

Islam is an urban religion, which developed and sought to create a new society in opposition to the tribes of the desert. In the Qur'an the 'Arabs', meaning here the nomads, are cast as unreliable, and in need of subjugation. The Prophet Muhammad himself was a merchant who, unlike his Christian counterpart Jesus, enjoined no cult of austerity or self-imposed deprivation, and believed in creating a strong state. One of the prime functions of the legal system he began, which later came to be known as *shari'ah*, was to base the legal codes of the new urban faith on the more fluid tribal legal system, or *'urf.* (See also Myth 7.)

89

Islam forbids alcohol.

The doctrine and practice of the Islamic world on alcohol (itself an Arabic word) are rather more varied than this. The early verses of the Qur'an (16:67) permit the drinking of *khamr* (wine), and the Muslim paradise is famously described in the Holy Book as containing 'rivers of wine'. Throughout the history of the Islamic world wine, and the culture of drinking and festivity associated with it, have been recurrent themes, perhaps most notably in mediaeval Persian poetry where the pleasures of wine and love are praised and in the poetry of the ninth-century Arab poet Abu Nawas, who wrote: 'Bring me wine, and, if it is truly wine, then say that it is so.' (See *Poems of Wine and Revelry. The* Khamriyyat *of Abu Nuwas*, translated by Jim Colville, Kegan Paul International, 2005.) The mediaeval medical study by Muhammad ibn Zaharia al-

Razi (in 1012) contained a chapter on the benefits of wine, although recent editions have removed this. (On the role of wine in mediaeval Islam, see Peter Heine's classic study *Weinstudien*, Harrassowitz Verlag, Wiesbaden, 1982.)

90

For Muslim women, it is compulsory to wear a headscarf or veil.

This whole issue is surrounded with confusion, starting from the fact that not *one* but *three* variants of appropriate clothing are fused in the term 'veil': 'modest' dressing; the covering of hair with a scarf; and veiling in the strict sense of covering the body and face. Until recent times the injunction to modest clothing referred to men as well as women, hence resistance to wearing Western suits, shorts, etc (hence also the preference of modern fundamentalist men for loose-fitting garb such as the Arabian *jallabia* or the Pakistani *shalwar khamis*).

There is not a verse in the Qur'an which enjoins the covering of women's hair or head. Verse 33:59 advises the wives of the Prophet to cover their hair and 24:31 speaks of covering women's 'adornments' from the eyes of strangers, but the practice of compulsory covering of the head (*hijab*), let alone wearing the full veil covering the lower face up to the eyes (*litham*) has no canonical authority. Veiling of this kind was not associated with the time of the Prophet, but came in the ninth century with the Abbasid Empire, and probably reflects a pre-Islamic Persian influence associated with that dynasty. Of the five major legal schools of Islam, none enjoins compulsory veiling. This is a social custom that has spread with modern fundamentalism and a misconceived and illiberal 'identity politics'. Needless to say, the majority of women in the Muslim world across the ages, who worked in the fields, did not cover their faces and do not do so to this day. Full veiling is an urban and largely modern institution.

91

In the 'true', 'authentic', 'correctly interpreted' religions of the region, women are accorded equality with men, if not a superior position.

Since the late nineteenth century, there has been considerable debate within the Muslim world, South Asian as well as Middle Eastern, about the rights of women and the obstacles which existing social and patriarchal practice, but also holy texts and traditions, place in the path of these goals. One pioneer was the Egyptian Qasim Amin; more recently, Fatima Mernissi and Nawal El-Saadawi have written on the subject, as has the NGO Women Living Under Muslim Laws. Similar debates have taken and are taking place within Judaism and in Christianity. On this issue as in regard to war, there is no one single message but rather a variety of claims, the priority of which is decided not by text at all, let alone divine derivation, but by the wishes and power of the interpreter. Some writers have sought to base a case for women's rights and equality on a liberal or even socialist reading of text and tradition, holding (in a form of argument with deep roots in Islamic tradition) that where one verse or saying conflicts with another the preferred one is said, by a process of supersession or *naskh*, to prevail over the other. The criteria for *naskh*, and the power relations underlying a successful advocacy *and* implementation of such an interpretation are not specified. In other words, politics, in the broadest sense, decides.

92

The Arab Islamic conquest of Iran in the seventh century imposed an alien and unwanted religion on the peoples of that country, something that has continued to oppress them ever since.

On available evidence, the majority of the people of Iran welcomed the Arab invasion of the seventh century as it rid them of the corrupt, clerical and aristocratic system associated with Zoroastrianism and the existing monarchy. Later, from the tenth century onwards, Islam, and the new syncretic language that arose from the merger of ancient Persian with Arabic, were to provide the means for the golden age of Persian literature and architecture, and Iranian culture and politics were to dominate the pan-Islamic Abbasid Empire. Later flowerings of Persian civilisation, after the re-establishment of a Persian state in 1500 under the Safavis, drew equally on a fusion of Persian and Islamic culture.

93

Before the advent of Islam, the Arabian Peninsula and the region as a whole were characterised by *jahiliyya*, or ignorance.

This is one of the central claims of the Islamic religion, by which all that preceded it in the region is cast as negative and unworthy of respect or recollection. If in particular it refers to the polytheistic religious beliefs that prevailed before Islam, hence the importance of the claim that there is only *one* God, it also covers the whole range of civilisations, states, cultures, languages and political systems that had existed in the Arabian Peninsula for at least one and a half millennia, notably the southwest Arabian kingdoms of Humyar, Saba and Qataba, and the Nabatean culture that existed in the northeast. The term also disparages the very rich oral poetic culture that arose in the centuries immediately before the rise of Islam. In modern political parlance the term has been used, variously, to denounce existing but corrupt Arab regimes, as by the Egyptian Muslim fundamentalist Sayyid Qutb, or, as in the rhetoric of Iranian leaders, to condemn nationalist and sectarian enemies like the Taliban in Afghanistan.

In any event, this depreciation of the pre-Islamic past has been ignored by every Middle Eastern Islamic state, with the exception of Saudi Arabia: the Egyptians invoke the Pharaonic period; the Iraqis, the Mesopotamian; the Libyans and Tunisians, the Phoenician; the Iranians, the age of the kings of ancient Persia. For their part, Israel and Turkey also make much of their ancestral, ancient, archaeological and, of necessity, invented pasts. In virtually all Arab countries poetry of the *jahiliyya* forms part of the school literary curriculum.

94

The historical truth of the life of Jesus Christ is based on the four Gospels.

The authority of Christianity as a world religion rests on the claim that a historic personage, Jesus Christ, was born around 0 AD in Palestine, preached the doctrine we now call 'Christianity' and died on the Cross around 33 AD. However, on the basis of conventional historiographic criteria, the evidence for the historical Christ is weak. There is no archaeological evidence of any kind that would support this claim. The main literary sources, the four Gospels, are of Christian origin, and so suspect, as well as written well after the events described. The first of the four canonical gospels to be written, that of Mark, was written in Rome about 65 AD, three decades after the death of Christ; that of Luke in Syria, some time after 65 AD; that of Matthew, in Palestine between 75 and 90 AD; and that of John, in Asia Minor between 90 and 100 AD. The first non-

Christian source to mention Jesus was the historian Flavius Josephus, who mentions the martyrdom of James, 'brother of Jesus, known as Christ', although another passage in Josephus mentioning Christ is thought by some scholars to have been tampered with by Christian scribes.

95

A Jewish state cannot, according to the Bible, give away Jewish land.

This is the claim of the religious nationalists who prevail today in Israel. However, as recorded in 1 Kings 9:11, King Solomon gave twenty villages in Galilee to King Hiram of Tyre, after the latter had provided him with cedar wood with which to build the First Temple. Galilee is indisputably part of 'Jewish land'.

96

The Baha'i faith, which originated in Iran in the mid-nineteenth century and today has around 6 million followers worldwide, is not a religion or faith but a political movement and should not be accorded equal status with other religions established in the Middle East.

This, although little noticed in the West, is one of the most abiding and pernicious of all prejudices in the Middle East. The Baha'i command a widespread following in Iran, where many tens of thousands of its adherents still live, and have strong following in North America and parts of Africa. Their total numbers are believed to be around 6 million. Of all significant religions, the Baha'i faith is the one that comes nearest, although it does not quite make it, to proclaiming the equality of men and women, and it also preaches a strong commitment to universalism, including inter-ethnic marriage. Yet in no Middle Eastern states other than Israel do the Baha'i have the right to public worship and organisation.

In Iran it is almost universally held, even by those of secular orientation, that the Baha'i faith is not a religion but a (British-backed) conspiracy. Tolerated, with occasional state-supported attacks during the time of the Shah up to 1979, the Baha'i have been driven underground by the Islamic Republic and subject to repeated vilification in public life, as well as to discrimination in state employment. The Islamic Republic accords official recognition and political status to three minority religions – Zoroastrianism, Armenian Christianity and Judaism – but not to the Baha'i faith. It is worth noting, however, that as of 2004 they have not been subjected to an all-out persecution or pogrom.

97

In 1989 the Iranian leader Ayatollah Khomeini pronounced a *fatwa* against the novelist Salman Rushdie in condemnation of Rushdie's novel *The Satanic Verses*.

On 14 February 1989 Khomeini did indeed issue a condemnation of *The Satanic Verses*, an event which led to the writer living in protected custody for several years, to the burning of his book in public by Muslims in the UK and elsewhere and attacks on his publishers and translators across the world. The reason for this condemnation was said to be the fact that Rushdie had, in his book, committed 'blasphemy' by satirising the Prophet, a transgression punishable by death within Islamic law.

There are, however, a number of problems with this account. First of all, Rushdie did not, in the Western, religious or legal sense of the word, commit 'blasphemy' understood as insulting God; the Prophet Muhammad, unlike Jesus Christ, did not claim to be divine – indeed, to assert that he was is itself, within Islamic tradition, blasphemous. What Rushdie was charged with by Khomeini was something more generic: *kufr*, which means denying Allah, being an infidel in a general sense.

Secondly, the story of the 'Satanic verses', which Rushdie told and which caused such offence, was not some invention of his but is an established mediaeval Islamic narrative as recounted in the writings of the famed historian al-Tabari, and designed to show that, while the Prophet listened to the angel delivering the word of Allah (i.e. to the words of the Qur'an which he then relayed), he was, as only a human being, capable of being misled by Satan, who whispered other words in his ear. The point of the story is, therefore, not to malign God but to point up the frailty of human beings. The particular issue on which Satan sought to mislead the Prophet, and ultimately failed to do so, was with regard to veneration by a rival tribe worshipping three female goddesses; Islam proclaims one God alone, this indeed being its central claim ('There is no God but Allah'), but in a mistaken tactical attempt to win over this tribe the Prophet was led, momentarily, to concede their right to continue worshipping the goddesses. The story is in no way derogatory of Islam and, indeed, contains an important moral lesson.

Most importantly, the statement by Khomeini was not a *fatwa*. A *fatwa* is a formal legal pronouncement by a Muslim legal authority authorised to rule on matters in dispute. It has to follow a certain format and, in the case of condemnation of books, has to cite the pages and passages that are deemed to be offensive. In Khomeini's statement there was no such format or citation; what he declared was something much less formal: a *hukm* ('judgement'), something he was entitled to pronounce but which lacked the legal authority of something binding on all Muslims.

On closer examination, this whole saga had little to do with Islam or holy texts, but was part of a political struggle by Iran to assert leadership of the Muslim world, like demagogy on Palestine. When the book was published in September 1988, no one in Iran took any notice even though Rushdie was a well-known and popular writer there, having won the prize for best Islamic novel of the year some time earlier for his critical portrait of corruption in Pakistan, *Shame*. It was only when, in early 1989, it became clear that political elements in India and Pakistan were making an issue of the book that the Iranians sought to pre-empt the campaign and take up the issue.

The Rushdie affair provoked considerable controversy in the West when a surprisingly large number of intellectuals and politicians criticised the author for having 'offended' or 'insulted' Islam. This was a rather strange reaction since, apart from contradicting the principle of free speech common to all – including the right to satire – it failed to note that in the Middle East, be it the Arab world or Iran, the intelligentsia refused to take part in this campaign. Indeed, the writers of these countries, in a variety of ways, made clear their support for Rushdie, not because of his novel in particular but because they could see, as the confused *bien-pensants* of the West could not, that the issue was one of freedom of speech in Muslim countries. On this see the outstanding essay by the Syrian writer Sadeq al-'Azm ('The Importance of Being Earnest About Salman Rushdie', in M. D. Fletcher, ed., *Reading Rushdie: Perspectives on the Fiction of Salman Rushdie*, Amsterdam, Rodopi B. V., 1994). Al-'Azm himself had been prosecuted for his 1970 book (*Naqd al-fikr al-dini* ['Critique of Religious Thought'], Dar al-Tali'a, Beirut) providing a sociological account of early Islam.

98

The solution to the problem of inter-cultural and inter-civilisational conflict is to build up an 'Interfaith Dialogue'.

'Interfaith Dialogue' allows of a number of interpretations. That clergy from different faiths should discuss their own beliefs and histories, and try to reduce inherited animosities between them, is clearly desirable, as is any role they can play in local contexts or at the international level to reduce tensions between their own communities. But such 'dialogue' may also serve another, less desirable, function, which is to legitimate these bearded gentlemen as the main or sole representatives of their communities and peoples, excluding not only secular, critical voices, but also those within their own faiths who hold different interpretations of belief and practice. This is what I have termed 'the Dialogue of the Patriarchs'. The result, unless countered, is that international issues and questions of belief and freedom of expression are monopolised by self-appointed clerics.

The basis for inter-ethnic and international discussion cannot be such a patriarchal monopoly, but a discussion on the basis of the universal texts and values which we already have, starting with the body of UN documents on human rights and the broader, shared values of the modern world. Not the least of the functions of such a discussion would be to invite believers in religion to participate, bringing out that in their texts and traditions which is supportive of modern universalism, while at the same time pointing out that *all* such texts and traditions contain elements which are, in any interpretation, incompatible with modern values. All forms of theocratic authority are in violation of the Universal Declaration of Human Rights and other internationally recognised statutes.

99

At the dawn of the new millennium, a 'New Middle East' is now in the offing.

Let us leave aside the fact that for most people in the Middle East, 2000 – a Western Christian date – is not the start of any particularly new anything. The call for a 'new Middle East' was a claim trumpeted by the US administration in 2003–4 when it carried out the invasion of Iraq and proclaimed a 'Greater Middle East Initiative' designed to bring progress and reform to Arab societies. The Middle East has been supposedly transformed by the crises, events and outcomes of many a previous year – the Turkish revolution of 1908; the colonial reordering of 1918–20; the founding of the Arab League in 1945; the defeat of the tripartite aggression over Suez in 1956; the Iraqi revolution of 1958, the June Arab-Israeli war of 1967, the Iranian Revolution of 1979; the Gulf war of 1991; the defeat of the Ba'thist regime in Iraq in 2003. Each of these dates has certainly marked significant changes in those who hold power in particular states, and each such change has had wider regional implications.

But continuity has, across the region, been stronger than discontinuity, with the exception of 1918–20. As for the history of reform, this began in the 1840s with the changes introduced by the Ottoman Empire, the *tanzimat*, and comparable changes in Iran, in response to external military and economic pressure. The region has, in common with other parts of the world, seen wave upon wave of reform – some cautious, some revolutionary – in the decades of the twentieth century, including during the Cold War, the rival projects of Arab socialism and the monarchical White Revolution in Iran. This historical record is not designed to deny the possibility of or need for reform today, or, but rather to suggest that any such project has to be generated from within the region itself and may take rather longer to bear fruit than the attention span of external administrations and their speechwriters.

100

The only thing people in the Middle East understand is force.

'Mission Accomplished.'
> George W. Bush, 1 May 2003.

'What we achieved in Gaza was something the Americans couldn't in Vietnam – total pacification.'
> Ariel Sharon, 1986, interview with David Smith, ITN Middle East correspondent, quoted in Smith, *Prisoners of God*, London, Quartet, 1987, p. 133.

'The situation in Chechnya is returning to normal.'
> Vladimir Putin, August 2004, two days before the Beslan terrorist confrontation and infanticide.

'The major military operations are now over and our armed forces are in full control.'

Sudanese President Omar Hassan al-Bashir, 9 February 2004, in regard to the fighting in Darfur province.

On the basis of the history of the region since, let us say, 1798, this proposition would appear to have been falsified. The people who only understand force would, rather, appear to be those involved in the region from outside.

A Glossary of Crisis: September 11, 2001 and its Linguistic Aftermath

All social and political change produces changes in language, and vocabulary in particular, but major upheavals and crises tend to accelerate this process. The history of European colonial rule in Asia and Africa, especially from 1870 to the 1950s, generated a whole vocabulary of domination, status and subordination. Equally, the decades of the Cold War, from the late 1940s to 1991, produced a wide-ranging vocabulary of denunciation, praise and place: 'running dogs' and 'fellow travellers', 'pinkos' and 'capitalist roaders', not to mention such now-forgotten places as Pankow, Peiping, Formosa, Algérie Française or the People's Democratic Republic of Yemen. The dramas associated with Checkpoint Charlie, the Bay of Pigs and Khe Sanh have gone the way of such colonial flashpoints as Fashoda, Agadir and Manchukuo. Terms such as 'stride', 'cadre', 'peace-loving', 'paper tiger', 'revisionist' and 'stooge' have passed into semi-obscurity. The verb 'to defect' has lost much of its force, as has 'to deviate'. Few now talk of 'Red bases' or 'Long Marches'. Equally few can define a 'McCarthyite', a 'Titoist' or a 'Browderite', though 'Stalinist' and 'troika' seem to live on.

This relation of vocabulary and phrase to political conflict was much noted in the twentieth century, most perceptively in the work of two writers – George Orwell and Victor Klemperer. Their insights are of lasting value and cast light, albeit under distinct circumstances, on the vocabulary occasioned by the global conflict over terrorism.

11 September 2001 and its aftermaths, in the countries of the West (particularly the US and Spain) and equally in the Islamic world, has had just such an effect. Hundreds if not thousands of new words and phrases have been thrown up by these events, some in the form of names and slogans produced by fundamentalists in the Muslim world, some by Western governments and some by the informal processes by which the public adjusts to a new situation. The following is one attempt to illustrate – in an inevitably fitful way – some of these changes of vocabulary and nomenclature following on from 11 September and to register the meanings of some of the words and names that the crisis has brought to the fore. It is necessarily a mixed bag, Islamic historical references sitting next to euphemisms of state from Washington and London. But beyond hopefully recording and/or explicating some of the terms and ideas thrown up by this crisis, it is hoped that this listing will, above all, demonstrate once again the ability of human beings to take and reshape language in the face of novel events. The list is by no means complete, and items could be added to it, from East and West, every day.

6+2. United Nations (UN) negotiating process, initiated in 1993, under which the six states bordering Afghanistan (China, Pakistan, Iran, Turkmenistan, Uzbekistan, Tajikistan) plus the US and Russia, joined a negotiating process to end the conflict in and around Afghanistan.

Abu Hafs al-Masri. Name of the head of military operations of al-Qa'ida who died during the US attack on Afghanistan in 2001, taken by Islamist group the Abu Hafs al-Masri Brigades, which claimed responsibility for the 11 March 2004 Madrid explosions as well as the attack on the UN headquarters in Baghdad in August 2003; the attacks on Istanbul synagogues in November 2003; and those in Istanbul on 10 August 2004, involving four bombs with two deaths and eleven wounded, among them foreign tourists. Also threatened in mid-August 2004 to 'burn' Italy if Premier Silvio Berlusconi did not withdraw Italian forces from Iraq.

Abu Qaqa. 1980s *nom de guerre* of Osama Bin Laden. Cf. Bin Laden.

Afghanistan. Literally, 'Land of the Afghans', denoting both all inhabitants of that country and more specifically the Pushtun. Founded in 1747 and ruled until 1993 by the Mohammadzai monarchy. From 1978–92 it was ruled by the communist People's Democratic Party of Afghanistan (PDPA) as the Democratic Republic of Afghanistan; from 1992–6, by the *mujahidin* alliance as the Islamic Republic of Afghanistan; and from 1996–2001 by the Taliban, as the Islamic Emirate of Afghanistan.

Against Islam. All-purpose excuse used by Middle Eastern and other Muslim states, as well as for patriarchs, clerics and other defenders of traditional authority, for discrediting critical or independent ideas. Examples include the Saudi government rejection of calls by liberal citizens for a constitutional monarchy; the Sudanese government's rejections of human-rights organisation reports on atrocities in Darfur; the Iranian government's denunciation of calls for freedom of speech in Iran; sundry *fatwas* or other condemnatory rulings by the grand *ulema* of Egypt, Saudi Arabia and elsewhere of views or interpretations of the Qur'an or Islamic law that they do not like. Cf. War Against Islam, Anti-American.

Against Normalisation. Arabic: *dhud al-tatbia*. Name for the campaign in Arab countries in the 1990s and 2000s against diplomatic relations with Israel.

Agent. Arabic: *'amil*. All-purpose term of derogation in Arab political discourse.

Akhund. Persian, of popular and often derogatory character, for a Muslim cleric. Hence *akhundism*, term used in post-revolutionary Iran by secular critics of the Islamic clerical regime. In English literature, the word occurs in the Edward Lear's poem 'The Akond of Swat', where it refers to a local Muslim ruler. Cf. *Mullah-ism*.

Aggressive Tactics. As in the US interrogation of prisoners at Guantánamo Bay. Often a euphemism for torture.

Al-Qa'ida. Arabic: 'The Base', or 'The Foundation'. The organisation headed by Osama Bin Laden. The existence of this organisation was announced on 23 February 1998, as part of a World Islamic Front comprising groups from Egypt, Pakistan and Bangladesh. The term has no apparent antecedents in Islamic or Arab political history; explanations range from it being an allusion to a protected rebel region during the communist era in Afghanistan; the Bin Laden family's construction company; or 1951 Isaac Asimov novel *Foundation* (first of a series of 'Foundation' novels), which was translated into Arabic as *al-Qa'ida* and which describes the destruction of a mighty empire, Trantor.

Amir al-Mu'minin. Arabic: 'Commander of the Faithful', traditional title of Muslim leaders. Taken by Taliban leader Mullah Omar; also one of the official titles of the kings of Morocco.

Andalus. Arabic term for Muslim Spain, covering eight centuries from 700–1500. Used to describe the political realm but also the literature and culture of that period. For a long time its capital was at Valencia. In geographical extent, much larger than present Spanish region of Andalucía, composed of eight provinces (among them Granada, Sevilla, Córdoba, Màlaga, Càdiz), with a population of 7.3 million.

In modern Arab culture, Andalus is associated with cultural

richness, religious diversity, science and architecture, hence use of the term in names of pharmacies, cafés, hotels, publishing houses and cinemas across the Arab world. Contemporary Arabic poetry and music retain strong Andalusian influences, just as Spanish *flamenco* (literally, 'Flemish') music, song and dance reflect continued Arab influence on its side.

The political claim, voiced on occasion by Osama Bin Laden, that modern Andalucía is in some way Arab territory that should be reconquered, is very much an eccentric, minority sentiment and has no serious resonance in modern Arab political history. The culture of Andalus and its contribution to the Spanish language and civilisation as a whole were long denied by the orthodox Christian narrative but, as part of a broader liberal critique of the dominant historical portrait of Spain, began to be questioned in the nineteenth century by a tendency (known as *arabista*) that sought to integrate the Muslims with Catholic history and the culture of the country.

The contemporary celebration of Andalus as a realm of cultural and religious tolerance may serve positive functions in the Arab world, as a counter to fundamentalist intolerance and hostility to influences from outside the Muslim sphere, but it also serves to confuse current debates insofar as it avoids the forms of discrimination (where inscribed in that system) against non-Muslims, as well as to make the often dangerous move of legitimating present policies in terms of supposedly perfect examples from the past – the trope to which fundamentalists themselves are particularly wedded. Recruiting an ideal past to legitimate current options (seventh-century Mecca, Davidic Israel, pre-Islamic Persia, let alone Anglo-Saxon Arthurian chivalry) can be a dangerous move.

al-Anfal. Arabic for 'booty' and the title of a verse of the Qur'an, often invoked by suicide bombers in preparation for action. Also the name of a campaign launched by the Ba'thist government against the Iraqi Kurds in 1988.

Anthrax. From the Greek *anthrax*, a piece of coal (hence 'anthracite'), boil or carbuncle. Since 1876, also a fever caused by minute, rapidly multiplying organisms in the blood. Treatment with the antibiotic Ciprofloxacin is regarded by many doctors as an expensive and more risky response than others, such as the generic drug Doxycycline.

Anti-American. In the US, an all-purpose term of derogation and denial of legitimate dissent. Cf. Against Islam, War Against Islam.

Antiterrorism, Crime and Security Act. 2001 UK law, passed in aftermath of 11 September and building on a 2000 law. Involves substantial curtailment of civil liberties, but did not go as far as the 2001 US Patriot Act. Cf. Patriot Act.

Anti-terrorism. Policies responding to terrorist acts. Cf. Counter-terrorism.

Anti-Zionism. An elastic term. In general, pre-1948 opposition to the establishment of a Jewish state in Palestine, above all within Jewish communities; since 1948, and especially since the rise of opposition to Israel internationally as a result of the 1967 war, denotes hostility to the exclusively Jewish character of Israel and/or to the existence of the Israeli state as such. Anti-Zionists would favour, in earlier times, a solution to the persecution of Jews within the countries of the diaspora; in the more recent period they call for an end to discrimination against non-Jews inside Israel and a repudiation of the claim that Israel is the home state for all Jews in the world.

The earlier forms of anti-Zionism came partly from religious groups who argued that there could be no Jewish state on this earth prior to the return of the Messiah, and partly from left-wing socialist groups who saw the solution of the persecution of Jews within the context of a European anti-capitalist revolution. Both these arguments rather lost relevance after the 1940s, the former because the state was established, the latter because the massacre of Jews under Nazism and the persistence of anti-Semitism in the USSR invalidated the aspiration to a socialist resolution of 'the Jewish question'.

While proponents of anti-Zionism seek to distinguish themselves from the racist ideology of anti-Semitism and articulate valid criticisms of the Jewish state based on considerations of international law and human rights norms, some of the rhetoric of the anti-Israeli movement in the Middle East and in the West contains anti-Semitic themes – for example, the argument (much-trumpeted since a UN resolution to this effect was passed in the 1970s) that Zionism is a form of 'racism' often contains such an, unstated, premise. That Zionist ideology and practice, like that of most forms of nationalism, exhibits elements of ethnic superiority and discrimination against non-nationals, is certainly true; but is equally so of Arab nationalism, e.g. in its Ba'thist form, of Turkish and Iranian nationalism, etc, and does not entail that these nations have no right to their own state – the underlying claim of the 'Zionism = Racism' allegation. Ditto for Chinese, Russian, English, American nationalism.

AQT. US military abbreviation used in Afghanistan in 2001 for 'al-Qa'ida and former Taliban' fighters.

Arab Street. Derogatory term for Arab public opinion, at odds with the reality that most such opinion is formed in a living or dining room, watching TV. Like 'Arab soul', assumes there is one monolithic public view. Cf. Soul of Islam.

Arabia. Elastic and often confused word, first used in classical Greek and Latin. English term for the Arabian Peninsula, in Arabic *al-jazeera al-'arabia*. (cf. *al-Jazeera*). The English term 'Saudi Arabia' is, in Arabic, *al-mamlaka al-'arabiyya al-sa'udiyya*, 'The Arab Kingdom of Saudi Arabia'. The older English term 'Araby' and comparable terms in other European languages can be used to cover the Arab world, as well as Iran, real or imagined, as a whole. Hans-Werner Henze's recent song cycle, *Sechs Lieder aus dem Arabischen*, translated as 'Six Songs from the Arabian' derives its title from one of the six items, a Persian poem by Hafez.

Arabian Candidate. Variant on *The Manchurian Candidate*, a Cold War-era novel (by Richard Condon) and film (by John Frankenheimer) involving a US presidential aspirant who uses anticommunist rhetoric as a cover for a communist takeover. In the words of American newspaper columnist Paul Krugman:

> This time the enemies would be Islamic fanatics, who install as their puppet president a demagogue who poses as the nation's

defender against terrorist evildoers. The Arabian candidate wouldn't openly help terrorists. Instead, he would serve their cause while pretending to be their enemy. After an attack, he would strike back at the terrorist base, a necessary action to preserve his image of toughness, but botch the follow-up, allowing the terrorist leaders to escape ... Meanwhile, he would lead Americans into a war against a country that posed no immediate threat ... The Arabian candidate might even be able to deprive America of the moral high ground by creating a climate in which US guards torture, humiliate and starve prisoners, most of them innocent or guilty of only petty crimes. (*International Herald Tribune*, 21 July 2004.)

Arabicide. Term coined by writer Fausto Giudice, chronicler of an estimated 200 cases of killings of Arabs in France in the 1970s and 1980s. See his *Arabicides: une chronique française 1970–1991*, Paris, La Découverte, 1992; see also interview in *Race & Class* (London: Institute of Race Relations, vol. 35, no. 2, October–December 1993). Cf. Genocide, Holocaust, Judaeocide, Politicide, *Shoah*.

Assertive Multilateralism. Neoconservative term for unilateralism.

Asian. Literally, any inhabitant of the continent of Asia, from Turkey to Japan, and comprising all of the Middle East, South Asia, Southeast Asia and East Asia. In contemporary British usage since the 1980s, an inhabitant of or person originating from South Asia, but of indeterminate religion (i.e. Hindu, Muslim, Buddhist, Sikh, Jain, Christian or other).

Asymmetric Conflict. Term developed by social scientists and US strategists in the 1970s, above all in response to Vietnam, to denote a war between fundamentally dissimilar powers – the orthodox state having an advantage in firepower and economic resources, the guerrilla opposition having greater endurance and tactical agility. The aim of the latter is to undermine the dominant state through political pressure on its regional allies and on its domestic, political and financial system. (For a classic analysis see Andrew Mack, 'Why Big Nations Lose Small Wars: The Politics of Asymmetric Conflict', in *World Politics*, vol. 27, no. 2, January 1975.) More recently used of attacks on websites and communication systems.

Ayatollah. Arabic: 'Shadow' or 'Sign' of God, highest clerical title in Shi'i Islam.

Ba'thism. A militant nationalism, drawing on fascist ideas of war, leadership and blood as well as racial superiority (in this case Arab) but also on communist forms of state and party organisation. Ideology of the Arab Ba'th Socialist Party, in power in Iraq from 1968–2003 and in Syria since 1963.

Backdoor Draft. Term used by Democratic opponents of US president George W. Bush in the 2004 election campaign to describe the extensive use of non-regular army, mainly National Guard and reservist forces, to garrison Iraq.

Bara'a. Muslim term for 'refutation' or 'denunciation'. While not one of the five core obligations of Muslim, this practice in prayers, sermons and meetings is considered a religious obligation and forms the justification for the speeches of political denunciation of the West which Muslim clerics are commonly heard to utter. Also used in the 1980s as justification for anti-American demonstrations by Iranian pilgrims to Mecca.

Battlespace. Pentagonese for a military and strategic context which their war planning will enable them to dominate.

Bazaar-Oriented Politics. Phrase of writers, e.g. the journalist Thomas L. Friedman, to describe political processes in the Arab world. Presumably quite distinct from, and inferior to, the horse-trading, gerrymandering, pork-barrelling, filibustering, arm-twisting, coalition-jostling politics, not to mention straight lying and corruption, associated with the electoral politics of much of the West.

Behind. As in 'Who is behind this?' (Arabic: *min wara'a*). Frequent response to a particular event, terrorist attack or assassination – with the suggestion, which may sometimes be true, of broader conspiracy or international connection.

Bin Laden, Osama Bin Muhammad. Self-appointed leader of al-Qa'ida. Born in Saudi Arabia in 1957, son of Yemeni millionaire building contractor Muhammad Bin Laden. Known in the 1980s as

'Abu Qaqa'. Attended Thagh elite secondary school in Jeddah, then studied management, economics and Islamic studies at King Abdul Aziz University, also in Jeddah. He is associated with the 1982 Sunni uprising in Syria, and with the funding and organisation of Arabs in Afghanistan in the 1980s. He returned to Saudi Arabia in 1989, but following a dispute with Saudi rulers over their response to the Kuwait crisis in 1990, he moved in 1991 to Sudan and from there, in 1996, back to Afghanistan. Cf. Bin Liner, Al-Qa'ida.

Bin Liner. Derogatory popular British name for Osama Bin Laden. (A 'bin liner' in UK parlance is a rubbish sack.)

Biometrics. Application of scientific methods to identification of suspects, using data on irises, fingerprints and face. Basis for US government campaign after 2001 to get other states to issue passports with biometric data. Biometrics uses a binary image to register such data. After 2001, major problems arose with this technology: eyes that were blue, watery or had contact lenses were registered inaccurately, as were those with Asian eyelashes. Biometric data also presuppose accurate databases which, in regard to irises, do not exist.

Bioterrorism. Came into use in the 1990s to denote the use by terrorists of biological weapons, e.g. anthrax, botulism, plague, smallpox. Cf. Anthrax.

Black Widow. Chechen woman guerrilla and/or suicide bomber, as in near simultaneous explosions on two Russians planes, in August 2004, days before the Chechen presidential elections.

Blowback. Evasive term, said to be CIA slang for activities carried out by former Western clients (such as Afghan guerrillas) who later turn against the West. Other examples of the exculpatory passive: 'the pen *was* lost' (rather than '*I* lost it'); '*it* slipped' (rather than '*I* knocked it over').

Boutique CIA. Term used by critics of the Pentagon to describe the Office of Strategic Influence, set up by Under Secretary of Defense Douglas Feith during the first George W. Bush presidency.

Box. Derogatory term used by US and UK politicians in regard to 'containing' Saddam Hussein. An earlier term, similar in denotation and tone, was 'reservation', as in 'X has escaped from the reservation'; this latter word originally referred to a confinement area for Native Americans. Cf. Cage, Come to Heel.

Brigade 005. A special military unit, composed of Arab militants led by Bin Laden, used for operations in support of the Taliban inside Afghanistan. Notorious for the violent suppression of opponents of the Taliban, especially the Shi'is.

Brigades. Arabic: *kata'ib*. Term frequently used by Arab or Palestinian guerrilla groups to denote their organisation, as in al-Aqsa Martyrs, or Abu Hafs al-Masri, etc. The term seems to have come into Arab political terminology in the 1930s when the Lebanese Christian leader Pierre Gemayel, influenced by Italian fascism and the use of the term 'phalange' (from the Latin *phalanx*) in both Italy and Spain, founded his own organisation of that name. Also favoured by the philo-fascist Muslim Brotherhood.

Busharraf. Derogatory Pakistani term for the pro-Washington president of that country, Parvez Musharraf.

Butler Enquiry. A bland and evasive oeuvre. A 196-page official British enquiry, by five people headed by Lord Butler, former head of the UK civil service, published 14 July 2004, into whether the Labour government had deliberately misused intelligence information in the run-up to the war with Iraq in 2003.

Cage. Term used by US and UK politicians in regard to Saddam, as in 'keeping him in his …' or 'putting him back in his …'. Cf. Box, Come to Heel.

Cakewalk. From African-American slang. Demented term much used in Washington prior to the 2003 invasion of Iraq to imply the supposed ease with which that operation would take place.

Capacity Crunch. Oil industry term for failure of oil companies and oil producing states to invest responsibly and with a view to longer-run energy needs in production and refining – a result in the case of the latter in tactical considerations of domestic politics and expenditure; in the former, of the domination of company decisions by the short-term demands of investors.

Capitulationist. Arabic: *istislami*. Term of nationalist and fundamentalist abuse for agreements that betray national interests, e.g. making peace with Israel. Cf. Defeatist, Tottering, Wavering.

CENTCOM. US 'Central Command', long based in Florida and set up after the Iranian Revolution of 1979; unit responsible for Persian Gulf security. Organisational framework for the 1990 Gulf, 2001 Afghanistan and 2003 Iraq wars.

Chaldeans. Eastern Christians, affiliated with the Roman Catholic Church, with substantial communities in Baghdad, Basra and Mosul. Protected under monarchical and nationalist regimes, but in 2004 subject to systematic arson attacks on churches by Sunni radicals, leading to mass exodus. The largest Iraqi Christian city has long been the American city of Detroit.

Chernishopi. Russian: literally, 'Black Arses'. Generic Russian term of abuse for peoples of the Caucasus, particularly Muslims – but also applied to Christian peoples of that region as well.

Chicken Hawks. Disparaging US term for right-wing advocates of military force who have themselves no military experience, e.g. Richard Perle, Paul Wolfowitz, George W. Bush.

Christian Zionism. The belief, particularly strong among Evangelical Christians in the US, that the restoration of the Jews to Palestine is a divine mandate.

Citizen Soldier. US citizens who serve in the National Guard, in the past typically a few days a month, but in recent years much more integrated into the regular armed forces and then used for longer periods of duty after 11 September to guard public buildings and generally reassure the public. Also known as 'Weekend Warriors' and, in Washington, 'Capitol Guardians'. The National Guard is, in fact, the oldest component of the US forces, going back over 360 years to the Massachusetts Bay colony. They can perform both federal and state roles.

Coalition of the Willing. Term used to denote UN members who chose to take part in a specific military operation without being formally instructed to do so by the Security Council. Polite form of 'posse'.

Code Orange. US Homeland Security term signifying 'high' risk of attack, one stage higher than 'Yellow', designating an 'elevated' risk. Used on several occasions after 11 September.

Cojones. Spanish: 'balls', 'testicles'. US political slang, applied by, among others, George W. Bush, to friendly leaders from other countries deemed to have courage. Similarly, the Persian expression for someone without willpower is *tokhm nadarad* ('he hasn't got any balls'); the Arab term *baydat* is used to refer to unflinching nationalist leaders – as in the frequently heard statement up to 2003 that Saddam Hussein, Osama Bin Laden and Yasser Arafat were the only Middle Eastern leaders with this attribute. In no case does it imply that the person so characterised also has any brains.

Come to Heel. Characteristic racist language of US columnists and strategists, treating other states and people as though they were tame dogs. As in article by US strategist Edward Luttwak ('America should threaten to pull out of Iraq', *International Herald Tribune* 19 August 2004), where he writes that if the US threatened to allow an independent Kurdish state in Iraq 'Turkey would soon come to heel'. Cf. Box, Cage.

Compassionate Conservativism. Bushite euphemism for greed. Cf. Haves and Have Mores.

Compound. Term generically used to denote fenced-off, private zone inhabited by expatriates in, say, Afghanistan or Saudi Arabia. One of the signs of serious escalation in the al-Qa'ida campaign against expatriates in Saudi Arabia in 2003–4 was its ability to enter and slaughter within compounds in Riyadh and elsewhere. Here the term denoted area of elite and privileged existence, in contrast to use in developed countries, where it refers to fenced-in areas to keep dogs, cars, etc. As distinct from its other meaning, to combine – which is of Latin origin – this is a colonial term used by the Dutch and British in Asia and believed to be derived, despite its Latinate sound, from Malay *kampung*, meaning an enclosed area surrounding a house. (For extensive discussion of this usage see *Henry Yule and A. C. Burnell, Hobson-Jobson: A Glossary of Colloquial Anglo-Indian Words and Phrases and of Kindred Terms,*

Etymological, Historical, Geographical and Discursive, Routledge Curzon, 2000 [first published 1886].)

Containment. Policy that had, allegedly, failed against Iraq, this being a justification for the 2003 military offensive. Originally used in the late 1940s to describe policy, formulated by diplomat George Kennan in his classic 1947 *Foreign Policy* article, 'The Sources of Soviet Conduct', for limiting expansion of the USSR and so provoking an internal crisis. Used, in term 'dual containment', for US Gulf policy towards Iraq and Iran in the 1990s.

Corkscrew Journalism. Instant comment, bereft of research or originality, leading to a cycle of equally vacuous, staged polemics between columnists who have been saying the same thing for the past decade or more. The term originated in the film *The Philadelphia Story* (George Cukor, 1940).

Counter-terrorism. Policies designed to prevent terrorist acts, if necessary by pre-emptive action.

Cradle. As in 'cradle of civilisation', an atavistic term used to suggest that all civilisation, religion, agriculture or whatever originates from the country in question.

Creation/Creationism. Controversial concept in both Protestantism and Islam, but with different connotations: in the former, associated with the conservative claim that the world was created by God at a particular time, usually 5000 BC or thereabouts; in Islam, it is associated with the liberal view, such as that of the Egyptian writer Nasir Abu Zeid, that the Qur'an is not an eternal document of fixed meaning but was created at a particular time and in a particular context and must therefore be interpreted according to different social concerns.

Creeping Right of Return. Israeli term denoting intermarriage between Arabs with Israeli citizenship and inhabitants of West Bank, Gaza or Arab countries. Used as basis for denying rights of family reunification when Israeli Arabs seek to bring their families home.

Crusade. From the French *croix* ('cross'), a campaign by Christians to defeat Muslims and reoccupy the Holy Land of Palestine in the eleventh to thirteenth centuries. First used in English in 1577. Associated at the time, as in the occupation of Jerusalem in 1099, with the massacre of Muslim and Jewish inhabitants. First used in 1786 to denote aggressive movements against a public enemy. The Arabic/Muslim term *salibi* ('Crusader'), has been used in recent times, but rather little before, as a term of invective against Western states. Its use by Muslims outside the Mediterranean is a product of activism in the late 1990s. Cf. Hulagu for contrary historical analogy.

CSO. Chief Security Officer. Corporate term introduced after 11 September, for an official with overall responsibility for a firm's security.

Cultural Aggression, Invasion, Imperialism. Common terms, developed originally in the 1960s and 1970s by anti-imperialist secular intellectuals, later taken up enthusiastically by Islamist leaders in power in Iran, and by militants out of power in the Arab world.

Darn Good Liar. Characterisation of George W. Bush during the August 2004 anti-war demonstrations in New York .

Da'wa. Arabic: literally, 'call', used for the call to Islam or to prayer, and then of political movements or parties – notably Hizb al-Da'wa, the Da'wa Party in Iraq, an underground Shi'i group opposed to the Ba'thist state and backed by Iran and later a participant in the post-Saddam political process.

Deba'thification. Removal of members of formerly ruling Ba'th Party from public positions in Iraq. Modelled on the post-1945 term 'denazification'.

Defeatist. Arabic: *inhizami*. Term of abuse for Arab states that negotiate with the US, try to make peace with Israel, etc. Cf. Capitulationist, Tottering, Wavering.

Defence Contractor. In post-Ba'thist Iraq, a mercenary.

Degrade. Vague US military term used after aerial attacks on enemy installations, e.g. those of Iraq in the 1990s, without making claim that anything has actually been destroyed or put permanently out of action.

Denial. Literally, to declare not to be true; in Freudian psychoanalytic theory, the denial of some form of reality, such as an unwelcome event or a particular trauma suffered by an individual. More loosely used in the 1980s and 1990s to refer to the refusal of individuals and collective groups to accept responsibility for their own crimes or for conflict.

Deobandi. A conservative Islamic movement, named after the town of Deoband, in India, where it originated in the nineteenth century. The ideological inspiration for conservative Pakistani groups, and for the Taliban. Opposed to the liberal trend founded by the college at Aligarh, Pakistan.

Dialogue. Much-used term to suggest open and respectful debate between different religious and/or political interests in the Middle East and representatives of the West. Often a pretext for officially managed theatrical events in which nothing of originality or independent character is said, serving to reinforce authority of state and/or religious officials. On the most substantive East-West issue of all, where calls for such a process have been made for thirty years – that of oil prices and output levels – no real discussion of an organised kind, between producers and consumers, has taken place: all has been left to speculation, and the market.

Dirty Bomb. Not a nuclear weapon, but a conventional explosive device combined with radioactive material. Cf. Nuclear Terrorism, Radiological Dispersal Device.

Disputed Territories. Israeli euphemism, designed to displace 'Occupied Territories', for lands illegally retained after 1967 Arab-Israeli war.

Do. As in 'do Iraq'; 'do Iran'; but also, 'do drugs', or: 'We do not do nation-building.' All-purpose, seemingly casual verb, usually betraying some barely suppressed impropriety in mind of the user. Cf. Nation-building.

Doddering Daiquiri Diplomats. Derogatory characterisation used in

July 2004 of retired Australian diplomatic and service personnel who wrote letter critical of Prime Minister John Howard's policies in Iraq.

Dysfunctional. Term used by the US Congress's 9/11 Commission report to refer to Congressional oversight of intelligence activities. Cf. National Commission on Terrorist Attacks Upon the United States, Global Intelligence Failure.

El Egipcio. Arabic: 'The Egyptian'. Cf. Rabei, Osman el Sayed.

Elevated Security Concern. Increased surveillance of airline passengers, public buildings, etc in light of information or intuition concerning possible terrorist actions.

Enlightenment. Process of change in eighteenth-century European thought associated with secularism, rationalism and cosmopolitanism, much abused in recent years by political theorists in the West. Islamist discourse tends to appropriate the term, arguing that Islam provides its own light (*nur*), and that enlightenment (*tanwir*) can be reached through religion. By contrast, in Israel, the Jewish *haskala* is now denounced by Jewish fundamentalists: hence the abusive use of the term by Israeli prime minister Ariel Sharon in his scornful references to the 'enlightened' (*maskel*) European states who appeased Nazi Germany in 1938.

Entity. As in 'the entity' (Arabic: *al-kian*), frequently used Arab nationalist term for Israel, avoiding mention of that country's name. Comparable to West German practice during the Cold War of avoiding the name the communist German Democratic Republic (GDR) by calling it *die Zone* (i.e. the Soviet Occupation Zone, its original post-1945 name); *die Sogennante* (the 'So-Called', i.e. 'GDR'); or just *Druben* ('Over There').

Espacio de Palabras. Spanish: 'Space for Words'. Electronic screen erected on 9 June 2004 in the Atocha station, Madrid, to substitute for altar with candles commemorating victims of 11 March attack, which was removed three months after the attacks at the request of people working in the station who were, among other things, affected by the smoke. Seven thousand messages were left in the first two days, and the daily number had not dropped below 200.

(Messages can be left on the Internet at www.mascercanos.com.)
As of early August 2004, almost 30,000 messages had been left,
among them:

> *How easy it is to kill, and how difficult to live.*
> *Amhara and Andrea, nine and five years old, send a kiss to all the*
> *people who are in Heaven, Mua.*
> *I do not know nor do I want to know the reasons that give the right*
> *to kill.*
> (*El Pais*, 'Palabras que llenan espacios' ['Words that fill spaces'],
> 4 August 2004.)

Ethnic Cleansing. Term popularised in the 1990s, referring to forcible
displacement of ethnic groups during conflict, initially in Croatia,
Serbia and Bosnia. Refers to practice seen much more widely, and
despite sustained vociferous denials by the perpetrators and their
descendants, in modern Middle East of Palestinians by Israelis in
1948–9; of Kurds by the Ba'thist regime in Iraq in the 1980s;
of non-Arab minorities in the wars of the Sudan; of Greeks and
Armenians from Turkey in the first decades of the twentieth century;
and of Turks and other Muslim peoples from the Balkans and
around the Black Sea over the nineteenth and twentieth centuries.
The word 'cleansing' has a sinister polysemic character, appearing
to stop short of killing or genocide, with mere displacement, but
also echoing the twentieth-century word 'purge' – a euphemism, as
in Soviet Russia, for mass murder. In all of these cases a significant
proportion of those 'cleansed' were actually killed, not least to
encourage the others to leave.

Ethnocracy. Rule by one particular ethnic group, discriminating
against those not from the group, as in apartheid South Africa, or
Israel.

Evil-doers. Old Testament term, much favoured by George W. Bush.
Cruden's Complete Concordance to the Old and New Testaments
(Alexander Cruden, Zondervan Publishing Co., Grand Rapids,
1999) gives seventeen references, e.g. Job 8:20 ('Neither will we
help the evil-doers') and Isaiah 1:4 ('Ah, sinful nation, a seed of
evil-doers').

Expedited Removal. British policy of deporting failed asylum seekers.

Fahrenheit 9/11. Film released in 2004 about US policy on terrorism and Iraq, directed by Michael Moore and 'quoting' earlier Ray Bradbury novel *Fahrenheit 451*. Enthusiastically critical of George W. Bush, breaking with all American conventions of deference to the president. While in his writings Moore showed himself to be a characteristic US anti-imperialist naïf (indulging, as many had done before him, the IRA), the main charges of his film (e.g. the connections between President Bush and the Saudi elite) were substantiated. (See Philip Shenon, 'Fact-checking a cinematic broadside', *International Herald Tribune* 19–20 June 2004.) According to the film, the president spent 42 per cent of his first eight months in office on vacation, instead of concentrating on a possible al-Qa'ida terrorist attack for which there was already precedent and anticipatory evidence. Corroborative evidence for claims in the film can be found at www.michaelmoore.com.

Fanatic. From the Latin *fanus* meaning a temple; one who is an extreme believer in religion and not open to reason. Term of last resort used by students of terrorism to denote 'new' or religious terrorists of the twenty-first century. A remarkably weak term on which to hang a general theory of this phenomenon.

Faqih. In Islamic terminology, an interpreter of *fiqh*, or Islamic law. In modern Arabic political usage, a verbose or irresponsibly unrealistic person, also a useless lover.

Fardh. Arabic: 'duty'. Islam distinguishes between *fardh al-'ain*, the five duties incumbent on all Muslims, also known as the five 'pillars' (*arkan*) of Islam, and *fardh al-kifaya*, an obligation – such as *jihad*, returning greetings or attending funerals – which is performed by some on behalf of the community as a whole.

al-Fatah. Arabic: 'conquest'; a term with Qur'anic resonances. Reverse acronym for *harakat al-tahrir al-falastiniyya*, the Palestinian Liberation Movement. Al-Fatah is separate from the broader umbrella Palestinian Liberation Organisation (PLO), of which it is a dominant member.

Fatwa. Technically, a judgement by an authorised Islamic judge, or *mufti*; more generally, any polemical point of view by a self-proclaimed source of authority.

Fiery Cleric. Alternative for 'wanted cleric'. Cf. Renegade, Venerated Cleric.

Fifteenth *Sha'ban*. Date in the Islamic calendar marking day in March 1991 when the Iraqi popular revolt against Saddam Hussein began, following defeat in the Gulf War.

Folks. Bushspeak for a terrorist enemy, as in 'those folks who did this'. Other examples of un-hegemonic West Texas judicial terminology: 'dead or alive'; 'posse'; 'outlaw'; 'smoke out'; and 'turn him in'.

Forum for the Future. Watered-down remnant of the originally much more grandiose US plan to reshape and democratise the Middle East. At the initial meeting in Morocco in November 2004, limited proposals were advanced. As a sign of disagreement, the king of Morocco himself left with his wife for a holiday in the Dominican Republic a day before the Forum met.

Fox News Channel. Right-wing American TV channel on the Fox network which gained ground in the early 2000s, with no pretence of journalistic objectivity. Osama Bin Laden was termed a 'dirtbag', 'monster', running a 'web of hate'. His followers were 'terror goons', and the Taliban 'diabolical' and 'henchmen'. Fox is owned by Australian-born media baron Rupert Murdoch.

Franchise. Term used to denote decentralised terrorist organisation. Cf. *Mouvance*.

Freelance Counter-terrorist. Private security contractors used by US government in conflict zones, notably Afghanistan, to detain, interrogate and abuse local people. Made famous by the case of Jonathan Keith Idema, an American freelancer who detained and allegedly tortured Afghans at the request of US officials, keeping a private jail. Press comment speculated whether he was a deluded mercenary or misled crusader (*Financial Times* 24 August 2004).

General Level of Arrogant Incompetence. Term used by British MP Gwyneth Dunwoody in December 2004 to describe treatment by US passport officials of foreign citizens arriving at US airports.

Genocide. Term denoting the killing of a people. Coined in 1943 by Raphael Lemkin, a Polish-Jewish lawyer who found refuge in the US in 1943 and single-handedly drafted the prototype Genocide Convention approved by the UN General Assembly in 1948. Although commonly used thereafter to imply the attempt to kill a *whole* people, as was the case with the persecution of the Jews under Nazism, 'genocide' also covers any systematic attempt through murder to destroy the culture or will of a people – including the selective killing of members of a particular class or professional group such as the intelligentsia. See Arabicide, Holocaust, Judaeocide, Politicide, *Shoah*.

Global Intelligence Failure. Term used by the 9/11 Commission report. Unclear if 'global' means covering the whole globe, or world, or involving all the fifteen or more branches of the Washington intelligence community. Or both. Cf. National Commission on Terrorist Attacks Upon the United States.

Globalisation. Term popularised in the 1990s to denote a range of concurrent international trends in three main spheres: liberalisation and increase of trade and investment in economics; democratisation and the increased linking of societies in politics; and the breaking down and intermingling of societies and cultures. Experts dispute the extent and distribution of each of these, their interaction and the degree to which the trends involved are a continuation of earlier forms of global interaction based on North-South inequality, going back decades or even centuries. Arabic renders the term as *al-'awlama* ('world-becoming'). Persian oscillated between *jahangiri* ('world-grabbing') and the more positive *jahanshodan* ('world-becoming'); the latter has, for the moment, prevailed.

Gloves Off. As in the phrase 'now the gloves are off'; used by CIA official at the Congressional hearings after 11 September. Implications include not only greater budgetary and political authority in Washington, but greater licence in the treatment of detainees and in the choice of who to work with in undercover organisations. Richard Clarke, former head of security at the White House, asked why the gloves were ever on in the first place, given the history of attacks by Bin Laden and his associates going back to the World Trade Center bombings in 1993.

God Bless America. Title of nationalistic US song, hence all-purpose slogan. Functionally equivalent to Islamic *Allahu Akbar* ('God is Great').

God-drenched. Term applied to speeches and policy of the American religious right.

Grand Strategy. Pompous term much used in Washington to describe and give bogus coherence to random bits of aggressive and bellicose fantasy.

Great Game. Used to designate the nineteenth-century rivalry in Central Asia between Britain and Russia, which ended with the 1907 convention defining relations in Persia, Afghanistan and Tibet. Loosely and rather inaccurately applied to the situation in the Trans-Caucasian and Central Asian regions after the collapse of the USSR in 1991.

Grief Gap. Term used to denote the distance between US and other Western reactions to the 11 September 2001 attacks, and the response in many other parts of the world.

Ground Zero. US Military term for point of impact on the ground above which a major air explosion occurs; first coined at the dawn of the nuclear age, probably first in print with a 1946 *New York Times* article describing the dropping of the atomic bombs that destroyed Hiroshima and Nagasaki. Now most frequently heard of the 5.5-hectare site and wreckage of the World Trade Center, New York, destroyed on 11 September 2001.

Groupthink. In the words of the 9/11 Commission report: 'collective groupthink'. From Irving L. Janis's *Groupthink. Psychological Studies of Policy Decision and Fiascoes* (Boston, Houghton Mifflin Co., 1972, 2nd edn 1982). Janis, whose work covers the disciplines of social psychology, history and political science, looked at what he termed foreign policy 'fiascoes': cases of spectacular misjudgement by US administrations, from the failure to anticipate the Japanese attack on Pearl Harbor (1941) through the mismanagement of the Korean War (1950–3), the failed CIA-run Bay of Pigs invasion of Cuba (1961) and the escalation of the war in Vietnam (from 1965).

In each case he ascribed the failure to the dynamics of group psychology, whereby individuals were reluctant to break from the assumptions of the group:

> I use the term 'groupthink' as a quick and easy way to refer to a model of thinking that people engage in when they are deeply involved in a cohesive in-group, when the members' striving for unanimity overrides their motivation to realistically appraise alternative courses of action ... Groupthink refers to a deterioration of mental efficiency, reality testing, and moral judgment that result from in-group pressures. (Second edition, p. 9.)

Ironically, there are strong reasons for arguing that the very reports produced by investigative committees in the US and in the UK after 11 September and the Iraq war, designed to identify the workings of groupthink were, in their usually bland and unanimous conclusions, themselves evidence of this process.

Guantánamo Bay. Territory in the province of Guantánamo, on the eastern coast of Cuba. Forcibly seized by the US in 1911 and subsequently used as a naval base. Chosen as site for detention of nearly 600 people captured during the Afghan war of 2001 and later because, falling outside US territory, it is not subject to US prison law. One of thirteen such secret or extra-legal detention centres worldwide. Famous in Cuban culture as the site of the popular song about a peasant woman, *Guajira Guantánamera*.

Gulf. Usually 'The Gulf'; waterway bordered by Iran, Iraq, Saudi Arabia and smaller Arab states. Site of over half of the world's known oil, and a quarter of its known gas reserves. Known for much of the twentieth century as the 'Persian Gulf', the region began to be called 'the Arabian Gulf' by Arab states in the 1970s, thus initiating a dispute that continued after the Iranian Revolution. Various alternatives have been tried, notably using the former Ottoman title 'the Gulf of Basra' or, briefly after the Iranian Revolution, 'the

215

Islamic Gulf'. The Kurdish writer Hazhir Teimourian has suggested that, as his people did so much of the work in these countries, it should be called 'the Kurdish Gulf'.

The frivolous and diversionary dispute over this nomenclature, like that over the three small Arab islands (total population less than 200) taken by Iran in November 1971, was a fine example of what Freud termed 'the narcissism of small differences'. It also calls to mind the observation by the Argentinian writer Jorge Luis Borges about the Anglo-Argentinian war in 1982 over the Falkland Islands (population 2,000): 'Two bald men quarrelling over a comb'.

Gulf War. Term applied to both the 1980–8 Iran-Iraq war, sometimes called 'the first Gulf war', and the 1990–1 Iraq-Kuwait war. Should also be applied to the precursor of both, the 1969–75 Iran-Iraq conflict, which ended with the Algiers Agreement between the Shah and Saddam Hussein in 1975. It was the renunciation by Khomeini of that agreement, in particular the commitment not to interfere in the internal affairs of each country, that laid the grounds if not the legitimation for the two later wars.

Halal. Arabic: literally, 'released' from prohibition. The Hebrew equivalent *kosher* implies something that is fit, or suitable.

Halal **Hippie**. Continental European term for European youth affecting an Islamic lifestyle.

Half-Jewish. Term used by people with a Jewish father but a non-Jewish mother, who claim a Jewish identity but are denied it by Israeli citizenship policy which insists on ethnic descent through the mother. A response to the orthodox claim that 'you cannot be half-Jewish'. The website of this name (www.halfjew.com) displays both testimonials from those in this situation but also denunciations of them by those upholding the official line.

Halliburton. Private US contracting firm which, as of August 2004, had earned US$3.2 billion for services to US forces in Iraq. Total contracts as of this time are estimated at US$18.6 billion. At Congressional hearings, former employees reported multiple malpractice, including failure to keep records of expenditure, dismissal of employees who spoke up, abandoning US$80,000 worth of new trucks on account of flat tires, and housing employees in five-star hotels in Kuwait. Cf. Sole Source Contracts.

Hamas. Acronym for *harakat al-muqawama al-islamiyya* ('Islamic Resistance Movement'), a Palestinian branch of the Muslim Brotherhood, founded in 1987. Also the name of a more moderate, and quite distinct, Algerian political party.

Happy Warrior. Term used for the US vice-presidential candidate John Edwards in the 2004 US presidential campaign; also, negatively, of presidential candidate John Kerry, as in a *Washington Post* article by Richard Cohen: 'No one would call Kerry ... the Happy Warrior.' The term, sometimes applied to Bill Clinton and George W. Bush, derives from an 1807 poem by William Wordsworth. (Thanks to American columnist William Safire's 'On Language' column for this one.)

Hasbarah. Hebrew term for mobilisation of pro-Israeli opinion abroad, particularly in Europe and the US.

Haves and Have Mores. Uncharacteristically shrewd and pungent term used by George W. Bush of his core voting constituency. Cf. Compassionate Conservatism.

Hawala. Arabic for a promissory note or bill of exchange; general term for system of informal money transfers. Also an Urdu and Hindi term.

Hawza. Senior religious authority of Shi'i senior clerics in Iraq.

Hearts and Minds. Term used in counter-insurgency operations of 1950s and 1960s, by the British in Malaya and the Americans in Vietnam, to denote attempts to win over often brutalised and terrified local population. Euphemism for propaganda, bribery and intimidation. Notably absent in response to 11 September and the run-up to the March 2003 invasion of Iraq, where emphasis was on use of military power (cf. Shock and Awe), but then reappeared in the face of widespread Iraqi opposition to the US presence in 2003–4. This is reflected in statement, of some historical condescension, by then-National Security Advisor (now Secretary of State) Condoleezza Rice: 'The hearts and minds issue is back.'

Hijab. Arabic: 'cover'. Conventional word for woman's veil.

Hisba. Arabic: literally, 'balance'. Term used in a variety of ways within Islamic law and thinking. On one hand, refers to traditional balance of power and influence within Islamic society, but also revived by conservative Islamic elements in Egypt to promote divorce of thinkers deemed unorthodox, such as Nasir Abu Zeid in 1992, from their wives.

Hizb al-Tahrir. Arabic: 'The Party of Liberation'. Sunni fundamentalist group founded in Jordan in 1953 by the Palestinian *sheikh* Taqiuddin al-Nabhani, which aims to restore the Caliphate. Has a following in the Arab world, Central Asia and Western Europe, especially Britain.

Hizbullah. Arabic: The 'Party of God'. A Qur'anic term revived in modern Arab politics first in Yemen in the 1960s then in Lebanon by Shi'i militants in 1980s. Hizbullah has widespread support in Lebanon and is represented in its parliament. In July 2000 it achieved its main strategic goal of pushing Israeli and Israeli-backed forces out of Lebanon.

Holocaust. Greek for 'complete incineration'. Originally a sacrifice, involving the burning of animals, as in ancient Israel. In modern usage since the 1960s, the term is used to apply to the genocide of 6 million Jews by Nazi Germany. Some historians have objected to the term on the grounds that it separates the massacre of Jews from that of other groups such as communists, homosexuals, the handicapped and Gypsies; and that it gives a spurious religious and providential, not to say fatalistic, character to what was an act of modern state mass brutality. This latter querying is distinct from 'Holocaust denial', the claim that no such genocide ever took place, or that the figures for the numbers murdered were deliberately exaggerated. Cf. Arabicide, Genocide, Judaeocide, Politicide, *Shoah*.

Holy Warriors. Washington liberal term for neoconservatives.

Homeland Defense. Taken from Soviet usage in World War II and applied to US defence policy in the late 1990s, to justify the National Missile Defense Programme. Since 11 September, it is has been used to denote US bodies responsible for internal security in general.

Homelanders. US term for core conservative voters.

Honey Traders. The cultivation and sale of honey are an important part of life in the lower Red Sea region, particularly Ethiopia and Yemen. There are streets in the Yemeni capital Sanaa devoted to the sale of honey. In Ethiopia honey consumption was, prior to the revolution of 1974, limited to certain classes. Following 11 September it was claimed that al-Qa'ida had infiltrated the honey trade and was using it as a cover for moving funds. Severe controls were, for a time, imposed by the relevant states on the trade.

Hulagu. Mongol leader who sacked Baghdad, and destroyed the Abbasid Empire, the second of the great Arab Islamic empires, in 1258. Term used by Saddam Hussein in 1991 to describe George Bush senior. Saddam did not, at that time, use the term 'Crusader'. Cf. Crusade.

Hussein, Saddam. Former Iraqi leader, detained by US forces in 2003. Born near Tikrit, northern Iraq 1937. Joined underground Ba'th Party in the 1950s. Was wounded and fled country after attempt on life of then-President Abdel Karim Qassim in 1959, then lived as a refugee in Cairo where he had regular contact with US embassy. Already important figure in seizure of power by the Ba'th in July 1968, from early 1970s he was in effect the most powerful person in Iraq. Formally appointed President in 1979. Led his country into two disastrous wars with Iran (1980–8) and Kuwait (1990–1). Careful student of Soviet dictator Josef Stalin. Believed to be the author of novels.

Said, prior to his fall: 'You may get rid of me as president, but when you do you will need seven presidents to hold this country down.' Also remarked to Kuwaiti visitor, in regard to strong Iraqi response to border incident with Kuwait: 'When a cat annoys you, you do not pull its tail, you chop off its head.'

Despite his arrest, popular in much of the Arab world, where he was known as *al-rais al'asir*, 'the Prisoner President'. See Said Aburish, *Saddam Hussein: The Politics of Revenge*, Bloomsbury,

London, 2001 and Kanan Makiya, *Republic of Fear: The Politics of Modern Iraq*, University of California Press, 1998 (new edn; 1st edn published 1989, under the pseudonym Samir al-Khalil).

Ijtihad. Arabic; from the same root as *jihad*; independent judgement in the interpretation of texts within Islam; especially associated with Shi'is. The conventional Sunni position is that the 'gate of *ijtihad*' was closed centuries ago. Cf. Jihad.

'Ilm. Arabic: 'knowledge'; 'science'. Root of conventional term for clergyman, *'alim* (plural *ulema*). In modern usage applied equally to what in the West would be theology and natural science. Registered in quotation of the Prophet, *'atlub al-'ilm hatta fi al-sin* ('seek ye knowledge even in China'), a saying often used to promote an open-minded attitude to ideas from the non-Muslim world, where China is taken – as it was in the seventh century – as the most remote area of the known world. Cf. *Mullah, Ulema*.

Imperial Hubris. Title of book published by ex-CIA official in the summer of 2004 under the name 'Anonymous', arguing that the US was losing the war against terrorism and that the invasion of Iraq had strengthened the terrorists' hands. 'Hubris' is the classical Greek term for pride, leading, inevitably, to a fall.

Imposed. Arabic: *mafrudh*; Persian: *mahmul*. Widespread term in the Middle East, referring to agreements, compromises and treaties that are said to be 'imposed' from outside, and hence to be rejected. Also used by Iranians to refer to the 1980–8 Gulf war, which Iraq initiated in September 1980 (*jang-i mahmul*, 'the Imposed War'), the implication here being not only that Iran was an innocent party but that in invading Iran the Iraqis had acted at the behest of Western imperialism.

Individuals of Investigative Interest. FBI term used in the summer of 2001 for Arabs pursuing usual training programmes in aviation and suspected – rightly, as it turned out – of planning a mass hijack of civilian aircraft.

Institutionally Annoyed. Term used by the European Union (EU) to denote disapproval by officials in Brussels of Israeli settlement expansion plans, without this implying that any individual government member of the EU had also expressed such disapproval.

Intellectual Author. Term used by Mariano Rajoy, secretary general of the opposition People's Party in Spain, to assert link between Arabs involved in March 11 bombings in Madrid and the Basque separatist group ETA. Minister of the Interior in the PP government at the time of the explosions, Rajoy drew on the authority of his personal experience to say that while it was Arabs who carried out the actual attacks 'these men do not have the intellectual capacity to prepare this type of action'. This argument was in line with the general claim made by the PP government immediately after the Madrid attacks in which they sought to place the blame on ETA.

Intelligence Data. Otherwise, 'raw intelligence data' or 'solid intelligence'. The assumption that there are bare, straightforward 'facts' or 'data' which are then, in some separate operation, liable to interpretation or analysis, is an elementary epistemological mistake. Cf. Raw Intelligence.

Intelligence. One of the most abused words in the whole 9/11 story. Supposedly secret information, often rumour, conjecture, innuendo or invention. Shrewdly contrasted by American journalist Jonathan Randal to 'knowledge' in his *Osama: Making of a Terrorist* (Knopf, 2004).

Intelligence-Industrial Complex. Term used by US intelligence expert James Bamford to refer to the use by the CIA, itself under staff pressures but with increased budget allocations, to contract out intelligence work to private companies and contractors, themselves largely staffed by ex-CIA personnel. Bamford speculated that there could be thousands of such people working, at a cost of hundreds of millions of dollars. He raised serious doubts about the competence, financial oversight and general efficacy of such contractors ('Rent a Spy', *International Herald Tribune*, 21 June 2004).

Interrogation Techniques. Term used to describe forms of interrogation and torture authorised by US General Roberto Sanchez, later commander-in-chief of US forces in Iraq. These techniques included manipulation of the prisoners' diet; isolation for more than thirty days, inflicting humiliation; deploying dogs; keeping prisoners in a 'pressure posture' for up to forty-five minutes; and denying the use of religious symbols. These were among the techniques used by US interrogators in the Baghdad prison of Abu Ghraib, site of some of the greatest violations of prisoners' rights during the US occupation of Iraq.

Intifada. Arabic: 'uprising'. A level of mobilisation below *thawra* ('revolution'). Used for the 1948 and 1952 popular demonstrations in Iraq and the 1970–1 state-directed peasant risings in South Yemen, but mostly associated with the Palestinian movements of 1987–92 and 2000–1 against the Israeli occupation.

Investor Reluctance. Mawkish financial press term for refusal of investors to put money into economies where the elite controlling the state robs the private sector and refuses to guarantee economic transparency, legality or stability.

'Iqab Allah. From the same root as 'sanctions' (*'uqubat*). Literally, 'the punishment of God', the phrase was used by Osama Bin Laden to refer to the 11 September attacks in the US, and was then taken up by protesting crowds in the Arab world.

Iraq Survey Group. Military unit, drawn from US and British personnel, set up to analyse mountains of documents and other material found in Iraq after the 2003 war and relating to a possible Weapons of Mass Destruction (WMD) programme. Based in US military base in Qatar, the ISG was much referred to immediately after the war as a possible source of evidence for the existence of WMD, but it soon slid into obscurity. One reason is believed to be that many of its personnel, translators and others, were sent to Iraq to deal with the deteriorating security situation there. On a visit to Qatar in February 2004, I asked the British embassy to arrange a visit for him to the ISG: 'I am sorry, I cannot help you on that one', the senior diplomat in question replied, professing never to have heard of the unit.

Iraqi National Congress. Term modelled, without much real similarity, on the African National Congress of Nelson Mandela.

Islam. Literally, 'submission' in Arabic, the religion revealed to the Prophet Muhammad between 610–32 AD. Now the faith of well over 1 billion believers, around 90 per cent Sunni and 10 per cent Shi'i, with some other, smaller groups such as the Ibadhis of Oman. Over fifty countries are members of the Islamic Conference Organisation, an inter-state body set up in 1969 after an arson attack on the al-Aqsa mosque in Jerusalem. The core texts of Islam are the Qur'an, the word of Allah as revealed to Muhammad, and the *hadiths*, or sayings attributed to the Prophet.

Islambouli, Khalid. Assassin of Egyptian President Anwar Sadat at military parade, October 1981. Later had street named after him in Tehran; one of many new Iraqi guerrilla units, also so named, is responsible for, among other things, the massacre of twelve Nepalese contract workers in August 2004.

Islamic Army in Iraq. Arabic: *al-jaish al-islami fi iraq*. Underground group that emerged in 2004, killing Italian journalist and anti-war campaigner Enzo Baldoni in August and demanding an end to the French ban on Islamic headscarves. Militantly Sunni and close to Wahhabism and al-Qa'ida, it is strongly critical of the Iranian role in Iraq and of Shi'ism more generally.

Islamic Art. As readers of the *International Herald Tribune* correspondent Souren Melikian's frequent and scholarly articles will know, this is a fictitious term without historical, artistic or theological basis, invented by museum curators and salesroom promoters to cover a wide variety of different cultural and geographic works.

Islamic Public. Term coined by the German historian Reinhardt Schulze to denote the growth, from the nineteenth century onwards, of an informed, newspaper- and book-reading Muslim intelligentsia, and more broadly a community of people in different countries aware of issues of common concern. (See his *A History of the Islamic Peoples*, London, I. B. Tauris.)

Islamism. Term used as an alternative to 'fundamentalist' and the French *intégriste*, to denote a movement that used a return to a supposedly traditional Islam as the basis for a radical political programme. Examples would include the Iranian Revolution, the Muslim Brotherhood, Deobandism and the Taliban.

Jackson, Robert. Forty-four-year old American kidnapped and shot in Riyadh, Saudi Arabia, in June 2004. His captors stated that they had killed him for working with the American arm firm Vinnell, manufacturers of the Apache helicopter used against rebels in Iraq.

Jahiliyya. Arabic: 'ignorance'. Generic Qur'anic term for the time before the arrival of Islam. Used in modern times by fundamentalists to denote secular Arab rulers and the non-Muslim, specifically Western, world.

al-Jazeera. Arabic: 'island'; 'peninsula'. Conventional word for the Arabian Peninsula, or what in English, but not in Arabic, is termed 'Arabia'. Used as a name for the pan-Arab satellite TV station based in Qatar since 1996.

As *jazirat Muhammad* ('the peninsula of [the Prophet] Muhammad'), also used by Osama Bin Laden for Saudi Arabia, whose name he rejects. The use of this inclusive term by the al-Qa'ida leader would seem to imply first that *all* of the Arabian Peninsula is one territory, with no distinction between Saudi Arabia – which is four-fifths of the territory – and the other six states (Yemen, Kuwait, Oman, Bahrain, Qatar and the United Arab Emirates); and secondly, that the whole of this territory, not just the holy cities of Mecca and Medina and their environs, is sacred (cf. Mecca). The former assumption is seen by non-Saudis as an expression of expansionism; the latter has no legal or scriptural foundation.

Jenin Martyrs Brigades. Radical Palestinian group based in the al-Bureik refugee camp in Gaza. Takes its name from a camp on the West Bank that was site of a particularly brutal Israeli-Palestinian confrontation in 2001. Took part in the July 2004 uprising against local police and other Palestinian Authority officials which challenged the authority of Yasser Arafat.

Jerusalem. From the Hebrew *ir ha-shalom* ('city of peace'); claimed by both Israel and Palestine as their political capital. The Arabic name for the city, al-Quds ('the blessed') corresponds to the ancient Hebrew *ir ha-kodesh* ('the holy city').

Another political term that can mean a number of different things, the geographical area it denotes has expanded greatly in modern times from the small historical centre – site of Christian, Jewish and Muslim shrines – to the greater city and suburbs of today. The religious significance of this city for all three religions has ebbed and flowed over past centuries; it is, above all, a function of contemporary political concerns.

Jihad. Arabic: 'effort', comprising military, political and spiritual activities. Normally used by Islamists for 'struggle', in contrast to the Arabic secular term *nidal*. From this root come both *mujahid*, one who struggles for Islam in one way or another – in modern terms a political and military activist – and *ijtihad*, independent judgement within Islam. Cf. *Ijtihad, Mujahid.*

Judaeocide. Literally, 'the killing of Jews'. Term sometimes used parallel with, and sometimes as an alternative to, 'Holocaust'. Cf. Arabicide, Genocide, Holocaust, Politicide, *Shoah.*

Kemalism. Ideology of Mustafa Kemal Pasha, 'Atatürk' ('Father of the Turks'), after the establishment of the Turkish Republic in 1923 as a secular and unitary state. The six pillars of Kemalism are: republicanism; populism; nationalism; secularism (Turkish: *laiklik,* from the French *laïcité*); statism; and revolutionism. Kemalism remains the ideology of the Turkish state and military to this day, contested by Islamist parties and Kurdish opponents alike.

Kharshi. Town in Uzbekistan used by US forces for operations in Afghanistan and Central Asia. Generally held to be the reason for US indulgence of the dictatorial activities of Uzbek president Islam Karimov's regime, in the name of the war against terrorism.

Kingdom of Heaven. Twentieth-Century Fox film, shot in 2004 and budgeted for US$130 million, on the twelfth-century Crusades. Characters include historical figures such as the Muslim leader Saladin (a Kurd) and Balian of Ibelin, the Crusader who defended Jerusalem in 1187. Arab Anti-Discrimination Committee spokespeople protested against the film as reinforcing anti-Arab prejudice, while an interfaith educational expert said it was 'stirring up a hornets' nest'. Director Ridley Scott denied this, saying: 'There's no stomping on the Koran, none of that.' (*International Herald Tribune*, 19 August 2004.)

Kongra-Gel. Congress of the People of Kurdistan: the new name adopted by the former Kurdistan Workers' Party (PKK). A ceasefire instituted in 1999 was ended by this organisation in June 2004, but despite Turkish government claims to the effect that it was the Kongra-Gel that was responsible for the August 2004 hotel bombings in Istanbul, most evidence suggested it was Islamists (cf. Abu Hafs al-Masri), or even part of a war between different criminal groups.

Kufr. General Arabic term for disbelief, used in the Qur'an for enemies of the faith, non-Muslims, apostates. Not a precise equivalent of the Christian term 'blasphemy'. Now used as generic term of abuse against anyone whose views the speaker disapproves of. One who practises *kufr* is a *kafir*, generally, an unbeliever. The word was taken by Dutch and Portuguese sailors in the seventeenth century and became a term of (European) racist abuse, as *kaffir*, in South Africa.

Lebanonisation. Fear that other countries in the Middle East, most notably Iraq in 2003–4, could fragment into armed ethnic and religious groups, each with fomenting external support as occurred in Lebanon during its civil war, 1975–91. In Pakistan, the 'Afghanisation' model is normally cited. European states were, in the nineteenth and twentieth centuries, haunted by a comparable fear of 'Balkanisation'.

Liberalism. Used in terminology of right-wing leaders of the Islamic Republic of Iran, as in slogan heard to justify closing of opposition press in 1979 (*marg bar liberalism* ('Death to Liberalism'). Meant to denote any pro-Western, secular or dissident thinking and activity. The term is taken directly from the vocabulary of Stalinist communism, just as are the Islamist concepts of imperialism, revolution and party (*hizb*).

Limbo. In Christian theology, a place that is supernatural, i.e. not earth, but neither Heaven nor Hell; a place of temporary lodging for souls that must purge their sins before being admitted to Heaven. In contemporary political parlance, as in term 'legal limbo', no such temporary or transient status is implied – rather a sense, as with those held by the US after 11 September in undocumented detention centres across the world, of being outside any judicial or accountable system.

Locations. US military euphemism for secret detention centres.

Magus. A Zoroastrian priest, practitioner of obscure arts, hence 'magic'. Used in Christian tradition to refer to the three wise men, *magi,* who visited Jesus at his birthplace in Bethlehem. In modern Arabic, an anti-Persian term of abuse, e.g. by Saddam Hussein of Ayatollah Khomeini during the Iran–Iraq war. 'Magian' is an alternative Western term for Zoroastrian and Parsee.

Mahdi Army. Arabic: *jaish al-mahdi.* Irregular Iraqi force, mainly recruited from unemployed youth in Baghdad and core Shiʻi cities such as Najaf and Kufa, by clerical leader Murtada al-Sadr in 2003–4. Used to stage high-risk, theatrical seizure of Imam Ali mosque in Najaf in July 2004.

Mainlining. Originally a term for injection of narcotics into the blood, used in run-up to 2003 Gulf war by US officials to denote the inclusion of suspect Iraqi opposition material in the official intelligence process.

Mamluk. Arabic: literally, 'owned'. In contemporary usage, often applied to Arab state reliance on Western advisors and specialists, this taken as a fateful weakening of initiative and independence. Historically a term for the special corps of Turkish soldiers and administrators, raised as slaves, who were brought in by the Abbasid Empire – a process leading to the gradual weakening of Arab control and the rise of the Ottomans.

Marxism-Darwinism. Term coined by Mexican novelist Carlos Fuentes to describe the policy of George W. Bush's administration; a combination of belief in an inevitable and emancipatory economic process, with a cult of survival of the fittest.

Mastermind. As with Osama Bin Laden and 11 September in or *El Egipcio* and 11 March, for example, the term implies that acts of terror can be understood like bank robberies. Suggests not only that there is one major organiser, but that the act can be seen as a manipulation of other participants, thus avoiding the unwelcome reality that there is considerable support for and willingness to participate in such activities among young radical Muslims.

Mecca. Arabic: *Makka al-mukarrama* ('blessed Mecca'). An ancient trading and pilgrimage city in the Hijaz, Western Saudi Arabia, population 700,000 (in 2000). Site of the Ka'ba (Arabic: literally, 'cube'), a stone covered with black cloth which stands at the centre of the Great Mosque, allegedly built by Adam and later rebuilt by Abraham and Isaac as a replica of God's house. The pilgrimage to Mecca, *hajj*, to be undertaken at least once in a lifetime by every fit Muslim, is one of the five duties or pillars (*arkan*) of Islam. The city has an exclusion radius of around 30 kilometres, within which access is now limited to Muslims. As a positive figure of speech in English, a place or goal to which people aspire to visit (e.g. tourist sites, dance halls), first used in 1823.

Middle East. Term first coined in an article by US Admiral Alfred Thayer Mahan in 1902 ('The Persian Gulf in International Affairs', *National Review* September1902, pp. 27–45). Attempt to delineate area between Mediterranean and India, also in contrast to Far East. Somewhat, but never completely, displaced terms 'Near East' (delineating Turkey and Arab areas along the Eastern Mediterranean), 'Levant', or, more recently, 'West Asia'. Generally includes the Arab countries of eastern Arab world, Turkey, Iran and Israel but, conventionally, excludes Afghanistan and Pakistan.

Despite its casual and imperial origins, generally accepted by all Middle Eastern languages, hence the Arabic *al-sharq al-awsat*, the Persian *khavar miane* and the Hebrew *ha-mizrach ha-tikhon*. Contrasted to 'Greater Middle East', term coined in regard to US policy in 2003, which includes Afghanistan but not Pakistan, and my 'Greater West Asia', which includes both of the latter (see *Two*

Hours that Shook the World, London, Saqi, 2001). Significantly, at a time when other geographical terms are being questioned, e.g. 'Far East', 'Central Europe', 'British Isles', etc, remarkably little nationalist objection to this term has been noted.

Mild Noninjurious Physical Contact. US military term used in official memo of January 8 2003, updating 1987 army field manual and detailing seventeen permissible interrogation techniques. Cf. Stress Position.

Militarism. Seemingly well-defined social science term denoting role of military concerns in society. On closer examination, has several distinct meanings: influence of the armed forces on government; high percentage of state budget spent on military matters; general public support for war; general public enthusiasm for belligerent and warlike culture; high social standing of armed forces in society; high propensity of that society to go to war.

Misguided Individuals. Saudi press term for terrorists.

'Mission Accomplished'. Statement by George W. Bush upon his plane landing on an aircraft carrier off the California coast on 1 May 2003. More Americans were to die in Iraq after this date than in the preceding war itself.

Mocilla Bomba. Spanish for 'rucksack bomb', used in regard to 11 March 2004 Madrid bombings. Related to *camión bomba* ('truck bomb') and *coche bomba* ('car bomb'). Term with particularly sinister resonance, as *mocilla* is also a conventional word for child's school satchel.

Mofsid fi al'Arz. Persian: 'spreader of corruption on earth'. Generic term used to discredit and, in court cases, sentence to death those opposed to the Iranian regime. Cf. *Moharib bi Khoda, Moser, Rodef.*

Moharib bi Khoda. Persian: 'waging war on God'; like *mofsid fil al-arz,* moral and legal term used in Iran to condemn opponents of the regime. Cf. *Mofsid fi al'Arz, Moser, Rodef.*

Moral Clarity. Term much used in post-11 September Washington to pump up support for simplistic historical and foreign-policy judgements. Often laced with quotes from suitably paraded authorities such as Winston Churchill and Woodrow Wilson.

Moser. Hebrew: 'informer'. *Halakhic* term used to condemn to death Jews who are accused of laying other Jews open to attack or danger. Used to discredit Israeli prime minister Yitzhak Rabin in the early 1990s.

Mouvance. French neologism, used for al-Qa'ida, to denote a group not organised on a traditional centralised basis, but more fluid and decentralised. Cf. Franchise.

Mowahhidun. The correct term for what in the West are called 'Wahhabis'. Literally, 'those who unite', in this case those (Muslims) who affirm their belief in the oneness of God. The practice of calling Arabian Hanbali Muslims 'Wahhabis' after the name of Muhammad Abdul Wahhab, founder of this religious tendency in the eighteenth century, is probably akin to the incorrect use of the term 'Mohammedan' to describe a Muslim – a result of the transposition of the practice in Christianity, where the religion is named after its originator, Jesus Christ. (That Christ himself, in his lifetime, could not have been called 'Christ' in any case, because the word is a later Greek term meaning 'the anointed one', does not seem ever to have bothered anyone.) Cf. *Vovchik*, Wahhabism.

Muhajirun. Arabic: literally, 'emigrants'; the followers of Islam who fled from Mecca to Medina. In contrast to the *al-ansar* (the Prophet's companions) who were from Medina itself. Term used in modern times by a range of Islamist groups.

Mujahid. Arabic; plural: *mujahidin*. One who wages *jihad*. Used in modern political discourse to denote nationalist and Islamist fighters, e.g. during the Algerian war of independence (1954–62), the anti-monarchical resistance against the Shah (1971–9) and the Afghan anti-communist war (1978–92). Cf. *Ijtihad*, *Jihad*.

Mullah. Arabic: 'master' or 'lord', similar to Hebrew *rabbi* ('my master'; 'my teacher'). General term in Shi'i Islam for a Muslim clergyman, or *'alim*. The South Asian term *maulana* signifies a respected clergyman. Cf. *'Ilm*, *Ulema*.

Mullah-ism. Pejorative but accurate word used in Pakistani politics by critics of the Jami'at-Ulema-Islami party, which backed the Taliban in Afghanistan, and of other clerical forces. Analogous to the Persian *akhundism*. Cf. *Akhund*, Muttahida Majlis-i Amal.

Multiple Intelligence Sources. Supposedly strong characterisation of basis for particular security judgement. Often reflects multiplication of chaff, or failure to evaluate differing importance of intelligence sources.

Muscle Hijacker. Person tasked with subduing passengers rather than taking control of plane.

Muscular. Euphemism for brutal, violent, at times illegal action against detainees.

Muslim. A person who adopts Islam. The archaic terms 'Mohammedan' or 'Mahometan' are inappropriate; mistaken analogies with 'Christian', a follower of Christ, they incorrectly suggest that the Prophet Muhammad was divine.

Mutawi'un. Arabic: literally. 'volunteers'. Enforcers of belief, the religious police known in Saudi Arabia and in Afghanistan as the Force for the Enforcement of Good and the Prevention of Evil (a phrase taken from the Qur'an). A brutal, authoritarian and intrusive irregular force used to employ dissident tribesmen and harass women, foreigners and others in public spaces.

Muttahida Majlis-i-Amal (MMA). Arabic: 'United Action Council'. Pakistani electoral coalition of Islamist parties, successful in 2002 elections, gaining control of two of the country's four provinces. In return to being allowed to campaign freely, the MMA then voted for an amendment to the constitution allowing President Musharraf to retain dictatorial powers until 2007.

'My Pet Goat'. Children's story from a textbook which George W. Bush continued to read for nine minutes at a school in Sarasota on 11 September 2001, after being informed of the two World Trade Center tower explosions. Famously recorded for television and featured in Michael Moore's film *Fahrenheit 9/11*. Cf. *Fahrenheit 9/11*.

al-Nakba. Arabic: 'the catastrophe'. Palestinian term for the 1948–9 Arab-Israeli war and the expulsion of hundreds of thousands of Arabs. In Israeli terminology, the 'War of Independence'.

al-Naksa. Arabic: 'the setback'. Palestinian term for the 1967 Arab-Israeli war in which the occupation of the West Bank and Gaza began.

Nation-building. Political term that confuses 'nation' with 'state'; should be called 'state-building' or 'state construction'. Originated in the 1960s and 1970s to denote the positive process of building state and other institutions in newly independent countries. Revived in the late 1990s and under the George W. Bush administration, first as a term of contempt for preceding president Bill Clinton's policies in Bosnia and Haiti ('We do not do nation-building'); then, after the wars in Afghanistan in 2001 and Iraq in 2003, used to describe US occupation policies in those countries with the suggestion that the military effort was being matched by a serious political commitment. Cf. Do.

National Commission on Terrorist Attacks Upon the United States. More popularly known as 'the 9/11 Commission'. Report commissioned by the US Congress, issued in July 2004; subsequently became a national best-seller. The report cited 'failures of imagination, policy, capabilities and management'. Listed multiple 'operational failures' of the US intelligence community prior to 11 September, including the failure of intelligence bodies to share information; check false information on visa applications and passports; successfully track two known terrorists who had entered the US in the summer of 2001; and include names of known terrorists on no-fly lists.

National Intelligence Estimate. US government evaluation, as in October 2002 regarding Iraq, of an intelligence issue or specific country.

Natural Growth. Euphemism used by US administration in 2004 to permit expansion of Israeli settlements on the West Bank. Part of general, if under-declared, accommodation to Ariel Sharon's plans.

New Terrorism. Also Superterrorism, Mega-terrorism, Nuclear Terrorism. Term used to distinguish al-Qaʻida and other groups from earlier forms of terrorism, e.g. the IRA, where means were more limited and some prospect of political negotiation existed.

New Thinking in the Law of War. Term used by George W. Bush in regard to laws governing interrogation of detainees by US forces. Part of broader attempt, championed by Defense Secretary Rumsfeld, to erode the Geneva Conventions of 1949 on the treatment of prisoners of war.

No Blood for Oil. Slogan used to denounce wars over Kuwait, Afghanistan and Iraq (both in 1990 and in subsequent years). Implicit is the claim that no humanitarian, or strategic, concerns lay behind the decision to launch these campaigns. Usually accompanied by facile denunciation of Western violence without any reference to the violence of terrorists and militaristic Middle Eastern states.

Nomadic Year. George W. Bush's term for his period of military service in 1972. That is, time spent doing nothing.

Non-conventional Deterrence. Israeli euphemism for nuclear weapons, generally believed to encompass around 300 nuclear warheads.

Non-judicial Punishment. Term taken from the US Code of Military Justice, Article 15, used to lessen or cancel verdicts handed down to US personnel charged with the torture and abuse of prisoners.

Noriba Bank. 'No *riba* (interest)', which is prohibited by Islam. Name given to 'Islamic bank' in the Gulf.

Northern Alliance. Loose group of non-Pashtun guerillas opposed to the Taliban, and comprising *mujahidin* who held power in Kabul from 1992–6. Mainly Tajiks and Uzbeks, their leader Ahmad Shah Masud was fatally wounded in an assassination attack two days before 11 September 2001. It is reasonable to surmise that these events were connected.

Not Part of Europe. Dismissive term, on a par with the rejection of an individual as 'not one of us'. Used to denote countries, notably Turkey but also Ukraine, Russia and the Trans-Caucasian states, whom some in the EU want to permanently exclude from membership in the union. Term demonstrating arbitrary and ignorant view of European history and borders. Often accompanied by suggestion, or acceptance in practice, that more distant lands such as Australia, the US, etc *are* part of the Continent.

Ignores the fact that the Iberian Peninsula and the Balkans were for centuries under Islamic rule, and that many of the core cultural components of Europe – not least religion, food and vocabulary – are derived from interaction with the Middle East, not to mention the effects of past decades of migration of millions of Muslims to European cities.

Nuclear *Souq*. Term used by American writers for Pakistani policy of selling nuclear technology to a range of other countries.

Nuclear Terrorism. Threat not generally seen as plausible before 11 September, but taken more seriously thereafter, whereby terrorist groups gain possession of nuclear material either to detonate nuclear explosion or a dirty bomb. The standard antidote to exposure to nuclear material is potassium iodide, but stocks of this in the US and Western Europe were, as of 2001–2, very low. Cf. Dirty Bomb, New Terrorism.

October Surprise. Term applied in US politics to events supposedly staged in October, prior to a presidential election scheduled for the first Tuesday the following November, that might in some underhanded way affect the outcome. Thus claims that in the 1980 campaign the Republicans secretly negotiated with the Iranians then holding US hostages to ensure that the latter were not released, embarrassing the incumbent president, Jimmy Carter, and allowing their candidate, Ronald Regan, to win. In the event, the hostages were released within minutes of Reagan being sworn in as president, in January 1981, but this could just as well have reflected an independent Iranian political judgement, not covert contacts – the existence of which, despite the best efforts of some investigators such Gary Sick (*October Surprise: America's Hostages in Iran and the Election of Ronald Reagan*, New York, Times Books-Random House, 1991) were never proven.

In the run-up to the 2004 presidential elections there was some speculation of another such surprise, such as the US detention or killing of Osama Bin Laden (this with the sometimes additional insinuation that if Bush had wanted to he could have done this much earlier), or an attack on Iran to divert attention from Iraq and Palestine. However, the only surprise – which, on the available evidence, had no impact one way or the other on the election's outcome – was the video speech by Osama Bin Laden broadcast a few days before the polls.

Office of Special Plans. This Soviet-sounding unit was set up within the Pentagon and intelligence community by Donald Rumsfeld and Paul Wolfowitz to push the case for a link between Iraq and al-Qa'ida, and to plan for the post-conflict situation in Iraq. Bypassed regular defence and intelligence bodies.

Oil for Food. Programme introduced by UN Security Council in 1996 by which Iraq was allowed to export stipulated quantities of oil and in turn, under supervision, import food and other necessities. Later associated with large-scale corruption within UN monitoring, purchasing and administration systems, and with systematic Iraqi circumvention of rules through a practice, known as 'the coupons of Saddam', whereby oil was given to foreign associates of Iraq, who were able to take a percentage of the sales in return for providing Iraq with unmonitored revenue.

OMEA. 'Of Middle East Appearance'. Term used by US authorities in racial profiling.

Operation Enduring Freedom. Term finally given to the 2001 US campaign in Afghanistan against the Taliban after abandonment of earlier versions, such as Operation Infinite Justice. (The latter was said to be offensive to Muslims, as Allah is the only possible source of such an action.)

Operational. Term used in a variety of contexts to suggest that some policy or unit is active in more than just principle, or to give strength – often tendentiously – to intelligence reporting. This word was used, for example, by EU officials to lend unwarranted reality to their Common Security and Defence Policy even when all it meant was that an institutional structure had been set up to bring the planned 60,000-strong rapid reaction force into being.

Other. As in term used in culture studies of and inter-civilisational relations, 'the Other'. Much used to describe European, and implicitly Christian, relation to the Islamic world, to support the argument that Europe's identity was historically formed in conflict. A valid term in the context of developmental psychology, to denote the process by which a child comes to realise its individuality and differentiate itself from parents and family, but usually misleading in describing relations between states and peoples.

First, a theoretical problem: in contrast to individuals, peoples and nations are by dint of being collective entities formed by a process of internal growth, conflict and self-definition, within which the external plays a second role.

Secondly, it is simply not true that European nations and peoples were formed through some collective confrontation with the Islamic world. Insofar as the external 'Other' played a role it was usually other European states, as in relations and wars between Britain, France and Germany and, for the colonial powers such as Spain, Portugal, Britain, France and the Netherlands, their relation to their non-European empires. Even in countries near and sometimes occupied in whole or in part by Arab and Turkish empires such as Greece, Serbia, Italy and Spain, the Islamic component of their identity and cultural formation is secondary at best. In terms of the history of international, i.e. inter-state, relations over recent centuries, the Islamic world was not the 'Other' at all but, as with the Ottoman Empire, a participant through shifting alliances in European diplomacy and, from the nineteenth century onwards, the object of colonial and semi-colonial appropriation.

Pain. Sentimental and often mendacious term used by perpetrators of political action, e.g. settlement of occupied Arab lands after 1967, to fend off critics of their actions, demand state compensation and generally refuse to take responsibility for their illegal actions. Those loudest in trumpeting their own pain are the most silent on the pain they cause to others, in this case the Palestinians.

Pakhtu/Pashtun/Pushtun. Linguistic community organised into tribes comprising over 40 per cent of the Afghan population, and that of the neighbouring North-West Frontier Province in Pakistan. Their main cities are Kandahar and Jalalabad in Afghanistan and Peshawar in Pakistan.

Pakhtunistan/Pashtunistan/Pushtunistan. Territory claimed by successive Afghan governments in Pakistan since the latter's independence in 1947. Afghanistan has contested the border defined in 1893, the Durand Line.

Pakistan. State formed in 1947 after the partition of British India into Muslim and predominantly Hindu states. The word itself is said, variously, to be based on the Urdu/Persian for *pak* ('pure'), or on the initial letters of some of the major provinces comprising it – Punjab, Kashmir and Sindh. An important goal of the founders of Pakistan was to free South Asian Muslims from what they termed 'Arab imperialism'.

Pariah. Tamil word for a caste that performs unclean activities, particularly leatherwork and shoemaking; later, 'outcast'. In international relations of the 1990s, term for states with whom the US has major security conflicts: Iran, Iraq, North Korea and Afghanistan.

PDPA. People's Democratic Party of Afghanistan, a communist party founded in 1965. Persian: *hizb-i dimukrat-i khalq-i afghanistan*. In power from 1978–92: leaders included Nur Mohammad Taraki (1978–9); Hafizullah Amin (1979); Babrak Karmal (1979–86); and Najibullah (1986–92). Taraki was murdered in October 1979 by Amin, who was killed by Soviet forces in December 1979; Karmal was ousted by Soviet pressure in 1986 and died later in exile in Moscow; Najibullah fell to the *mujahidin* in April 1992, lived for four years in the UN compound in Kabul and was captured, tortured and hanged along with his brother when the Taliban took Kabul in September 1996. From 1978–9 the party was dominated by the *khalq* ('People') faction, and from 1979–92 by the *parcham* ('Flag').

Perceived Liberal Bias. Right-wing American term used for the media, the term 'perceived' suggesting some validated or objective assessment.

Permitted Arabic Words. A list of Arabic/Islamic terms which prisoners in British jails are allowed to use in verbal communication with their families and lawyers. Prison regulations dictate that inmates may only speak in English, but some conventional Arabic terms like *assalaamun alaikum* ('peace be with you', the regular Muslim greeting) and *inshallah* ('if Allah wills', somewhat equivalent in usage to the Irish 'God bless') were accepted, through negotiation between the prison authorities and representatives of the Muslim communities.

Philadelphia Corridor. The land along the border of Gaza with Egypt. Israel has retained a military presence in this area, excluding it from its withdrawal from Gaza.

Polite Prejudice. Description of an indirect but pervasive anti-Jewish racism in Western societies.

Politicide. Term used by Israeli sociologist Baruch Kimmerling to denote plans by the Sharon government to destroy Palestinians as a viable political entity: 'This involves a politico-military, diplomatic and psychological strategy which aims to liquidate the Palestinian people as a legitimate and independent economic, social and political entity.' (*Le Monde Diplomatique*, Spanish edition, June 2004.) Cf. Arabicide, Genocide, Holocaust, Judaeocide, *Shoah*.

Population Centres. Israeli euphemism, increasingly used after 2000, to denote larger settlements on the West Bank, e.g. Ariel, Gush Etzion and Ma'ale Adumim. Designed to reduce the sense of these entities as being temporary or intrusive, and to 'normalise', i.e. make permanent, their status.

Positive Domino Theory. Neoconservative US view that the overthrow of the Ba'thist regime in Iraq would set off a democratic wave elsewhere in the Arab world.

Post-Islamist. Term applied to Islamist parties such as the AKP (Adalet ve Kalkinma Partisi, or 'Justice and Development Party') in Turkey, headed by Prime Minister Tayyip Erdogan. After facing such setbacks as the 1997 military deposition of then-Prime Minister Necmettin Erbakan, the outspoken leader of the AKP's precursor Welfare Party, the AKP moderated its ideological programme, foreswore violence and pursued power through elections and forms of constitutional politics. Instead of 'Islamist', the AKP termed itself 'conservative democrats'.

Post-Zionism. Critique developed by Israeli writers in the 1990s of self-justifying history of Israel in the 1940s and 1950s and of the Jewish character of Israeli politics and society. See Ephraim Nimni, ed., *The Challenge of Post-Zionism*, London, Zed Press, 2003.

Potential Marriage. Bush administration term for possible, but not actualised, alliance of Saddam Hussein's regime with al-Qa'ida.

Prayer Leader. Term used to denote person who leads the faithful in prayer in Islam. Not necessarily someone formally recognised as an *'alim* or *mullah*. Technically correct, and capturing original sense of word *imam*, which literally means someone who is 'in the front'. The task of leading the faithful in prayer can, in theory, be assumed by any believing Muslim.

Pre-emption. In US conventional parlance 'pre-emption' means taking action against an enemy that is, on reasonable evidence, about to attack, whereas 'prevention' means attacking an enemy that might do something in the future. The most famous examples of the latter are the US pursuit of nuclear superiority in the Cold War, designed to prevent the USSR from ever gaining parity, even while pretending that Moscow had 'superiority'; and the outbreak of the Peloponnesian War, when Sparta attacked Athens because it 'feared the rise' of the other's power (Thucydides). The current US use of the term 'pre- emption' is a misnomer, since Iraq was not about to attack, likewise Iran or North Korea. The term should be 'prevention'.

Pretzel of Preposterousness. Cf. *Triangle of Terror*.

'Prisoner Abuse'. Often euphemism for torture and war crimes. Term much used after revelations of US treatment of Iraqi prisoners in Abu Ghraib prison.

Private Warrior. Alternatively, Private Security Contractor. Euphemism for 'mercenary'.

Project for a New American Century. Right-wing think tank out of which grew the neoconservative agenda for the Bush administration.

Members included Donald Rumsfeld, Paul Wolfowitz, later, respectively, Secretary and Deputy Secretary of Defense under George W. Bush.

Promptings. Divine messages, as in claim by George W. Bush that he has been the recipient thereof.

Protection Crisis. Term used in August 2004 by UN officials to refer to mass rape and other forms of violence against the population in the Darfur region of Sudan.

Psychotic and Paranoid. Terms used in November 2001 by British Foreign Secretary Jack Straw to describe Osama Bin Laden. As some critics pointed out, he was probably confusing 'psychotic', a term referring to people who often suffer by extreme identification with the misery of others, with 'psychopathic', as the latter refers to someone completely oblivious to the sufferings of others.

Pundit. Instant media commentator. From the Sanskrit *pandita*, a learned man; specifically, an advisor on Hindu law to the British courts in India.

Qassam, Izzedin. Egyptian Muslim Brotherhood preacher and social activist, later guerrilla leader in Palestine, killed in 1935 on the eve of a popular uprising against the Jewish and British presence. As symbol of first armed resistance to Jewish presence, much invoked by later Palestinian fighters.

Qassam Rockets. Homemade missiles, manufactured by the Palestinian group Hamas in small workshops in Gaza. Made of long steel pipes, with payloads of 9 kilograms and a range of up to 7 miles. Used against Israelis living in and near the Gaza Strip.

Rabei, Osman Sayed Ahmed. Thirty-three-year-old Egyptian; former explosives expert, later trained at al-Qa'ida camp in Afghanistan; arrested outside Milan on 7 June 2004. Also known as 'Muhammad the Egyptian' or just, in Spain, *El Egipcio* ('the Egyptian'). Well connected with Islamist groups across Europe. Believed to have played an important role in the 11 March 2004 explosions in Madrid, having arrived in Spain in 2003. Said by some to have been plotting further attacks at the time of his arrest, possibly against the Paris Métro using 145 kilos of explosives and mobile phones as detonators.

Radiological Dispersal Device. Cf. Dirty Bomb.

Rais. Arabic: 'President'. Term used in the 1950s and 1960s of President Gamal Abdel Nasser of Egypt, then in 1990s of Arafat as President of the Palestinian National Authority. Example of common practice of naming leaders with official titles. Another is Libya's Muammar al-Qaddafi as *al-akh al-'aqid* ('the Brother Colonel').

Ramadan. Ninth month of the Islamic calendar, a time of fasting and abstinence from sexual activity from dawn to sunset. Associated with family and social visits at nighttime, often with special foods. Also associated with some of the bloodiest battles in early Islamic history, notably that of 'Operation Badr', the Egyptian offensive in the October 1973 Arab-Israeli war, and with heavy fighting in the Iran-Iraq war of 1980–8.

Ranger. Pre-1776 term for a US irregular soldier, now used for special intervention forces. Not the exact equivalent of the UK's SAS, as they are more numerous, less elite.

Raspberry. As in the British phrase 'to blow a raspberry', meaning to voice considerable scepticism about something; roughly equivalent to the US term 'Bronx cheer'. Used by British government official John Morrison, advisor to the parliamentary Intelligence and Security Committee (ISC), to describe his reaction to Prime Minister Tony Blair's claim that Iraq posed a 'serious and current threat' to the UK. Morrison was later quoted by the BBC as saying: 'When I heard him using these words, I could almost hear the collective raspberry going up around Whitehall.' After the broadcast of this programme, Morrison's contract with the ISC was not renewed, and he was given ninety days to leave.

Raw Intelligence. As any student of the philosophy of social science knows, there is no such thing as a 'pure' fact, or 'raw' intelligence. Nevertheless, this apparently clear term is used for information obtained by intelligence services prior to being analysed or presented in a report to political leaders.

Rearrange Wiring Diagrams. Term used to denote unwelcome and elaborate plans to restructure Washington intelligence community, and in particular to break up or demote the CIA, in the wake of the 9/11 Commission report and other official investigations.

Reconnaissance Plans. Term used in counter-terrorism to denote actions by suspected or known terrorists involving reconnoitring possible targets, collecting photographs, maps, videos and other relevant information. Also associated with form of intimidation practised by such groups, e.g. the IRA, when not actually intending to carry out armed actions.

Refusenik. Israeli term for potential military recruits who refuse to serve in the West Bank and Gaza and are, after hearings before tribunals, sentenced to periods in prison. Distinct from avoiders, recruits who fail to report for service on grounds – real or fabricated – of ill health. The usage of the term is derived from, but not equivalent to, the original usage from the USSR of the 1970s, *otkazniki*, to denote Russian Jews who wished to emigrate to Israel and who, after being refused exit visas, were then denied employment and subject to other forms of persecution. Direct flights between the USSR and Israel, carrying Jews who wished to emigrate, began only in October 1991, after the failed August coup in Moscow.

Regime Change. Neoconservative term for removal of hostile governments, somewhat derived from fall of communism in Eastern Europe 1989–91.

Rendition. In post-11 September US military usage, the sending of suspected terrorist prisoners to third countries without judicial process and with the knowledge that those countries routinely use torture in interrogation.

Renegade. As in 'renegade cleric'; alternatively, 'wanted' and 'radical'. Terms variously applied to Iraqi Shi'i extremist Murtada al-Sadr. 'Renegade', in origin a Portuguese word, is a term of colonial derogation referring to an escaped slave, later much used in the US in the nineteenth century to denote Native Americans who refused to accept settler control. Cf. Fiery Cleric, Venerated Cleric.

Right of Return. Right written into Israeli law in 1951 allowing all Jews to acquire Israeli citizenship. Later taken by Palestinians to assert their right to return to the areas of Israel from which they or their families had originally come.

Rodef. Hebrew: 'pursuer'. Word of religious derogation, used to denounce Jews who stray outside the faith and are, thereby, liable to be killed. Used in the early 1990s to attack Prime Minister Yitzhak Rabin and incite his assassination.

Sahel Plan. US training programme, initiated in 2004, to combat terrorism in North Africa. Covers Chad, Mali, Mauritania and Niger, with the participation of Morocco, Tunisia and Algeria. The aim is to build preventive barriers across Africa.

al-Sakina. Arabic: 'harmony'; oneness with Allah, suggestive of a mystical and possibly sacrificial state; used by Islamic youth training groups in the UK.

Salafi Group of Prayer and Combat. Main fundamentalist terrorist group in Algeria, result of split in 1998 in the other main force, the Armed Islamic Group (GIA). 2003 proclaimed itself affiliated with al-Qaʻida and called for *jihad* with aim of establishing an Islamic republic in Algeria. While the GIA indiscriminately attacked civilian and military targets, the SGPC focused on military targets initially, but then took to kidnapping foreigners working in Algeria.

An estimated 150,000 people are believed to have died in Algeria after the outbreak of fighting between Islamists and the military government in 1991. The group suffered a possibly major blow when, in June 2004, its supposed leader Nabil Sahrawi and five other leaders were killed by government forces in the Kabyle region.

Salafis. The Salafiyya was a movement founded in the late nineteenth century that revered the 'pious ancestors' (*salaf al-salihin*), of Islam. Originally a term denoting modernising trends associated with Islamic reformers Jamal al-Din al-Afghani and Muhammad Abduh, from the 1970s onwards it came to denote a conservative Islamist trend in the Arab world, especially in the Arabian Peninsula.

Salman Pak. Town near Baghdad said to house Iraqi nuclear facilities, repeatedly attacked by Western air forces. Named after Salman al-Farisi, a close *ansar* (companion) of the Prophet Muhammad and the first Persian to convert to Islam, who is buried there.

Saudisation. Also Bahrainisation, Emiratisation, Omanisation. Terms used to describe policies of replacing foreign with domestic nationals in the labour market. Despite much promotion by the states of such changes, local, and foreign businesses in the region have resisted this process.

Secret Detention Centres. In July 2004 the US was accused by the NGO Human Rights First of having thirteen secret centres around the world where prisoners are held in violation of the Geneva Conventions. These include Guantánamo Bay in Cuba, Abu Ghraib in Iraq, Bagram in Afghanistan, the Indian Ocean island of Diego García, sites in Jordan and Pakistan and at least two naval vessels off the US coast. Between 1,000 and 3,000 people are believed to be held in these places.

Secular Fundamentalists. Term used by religious activists in the US and elsewhere to discredit their critics.

Security Fence. Israeli term for the wall built by the Sharon government in 2003–4. Cf. Separation Barrier.

Self-hating Jew. Term with spurious psychoanalytic undertones, often applied to Jewish writers who criticise either elements in Jewish religious and social traditions or the activities of the Israeli state. Was applied, for example, in the 1960s against the writers Isaac Deutscher and Maxime Rodinson, Marxists who defended the case for an Israeli state side by side with a Palestinian one, but who denounced the religious and military fervour that gripped Israeli in the 1967 war; they also condemned the denial of Palestinian rights.

Similar derogatory terms designed to deny legitimacy to critics of religious or national communities from which they come can be found in other cultures and contexts – e.g., in the Irish case, the use of terms such as 'Castle Catholic', and 'West Brit', to describe critics of Irish nationalism; or the many terms used in Arab politics to discredit critics, like *munafiq* ('hypocrite') or 'Fuad Ajami' (after the Lebanese-American academic who has been a policy advisor and public commentator in Washington.

Selling the Threat. Closely linked to the concept of 'threat inflation'. Process by which governments seek to mobilise public support for military action by promoting alarmist analyses. In this case, the actions taken by the US and UK governments to mobilise support for the 2003 Iraq war.

Separation Barrier. Israeli term for the concrete barrier erected in 2003–4, encroaching into the West Bank and Gaza. Known in Arabic as 'The Wall'. Cf. Security Fence.

Serious Doubts. British official term for complete disbelief, as in the report by the Butler Committee on MI6's disquiet regarding the agents it had in place in Iraq prior to the invasion of March 2003.

Sexed-up. Mawkish British official term on threat inflation and exaggeration of intelligence material. Used by BBC reporter Andrew Gilligan in a 2002 report claiming Downing Street exaggerated Iraq's WMD potential. Implies that the thing (or person) so treated is, like intelligence data, completely passive, an anthropologically improbable premise. (British weapons expert and Gilligan's source David Kelly later committed suicide; a subsequent enquiry by Lord Hutton into the circumstances surrounding Kelly's death brought the 'sexed-up' claim in sharp focus. The Hutton report exonerated the government and Gilligan resigned.)

Shari'ah. From the same Arabic root as *shari'* ('street'). Generic term for divinely sanctioned Islamic law, now a talisman invoked by fundamentalists without historical or canonical authority. Often confuses those eighty out of 6,000 verses of the Qur'an that are concerned with law and, by dint of being the word of Allah, divinely sanctioned with the broader body of Islamic law (*fiqh*). *Shari'ah* is thereby used as a term to comprise the Qur'an, the *hadiths* (sayings of the Prophet), the *Sunnah* (records of the Prophet's deeds) and subsequent jurisprudence; these additions entail, however, that *shari'ah* is not divinely sanctioned.

Shell Game. Cold War term used by US officials to describe what they claimed was an Iraqi policy of moving prohibited military equipment and related documentation around from place to place to avoid detection by UN weapons inspectors.

Shi'a. Arabic: literally, 'faction'. Shi'is were the followers of Ali, the cousin and son-in-law of the Prophet Muhammad, who came into conflict with Muhammad's successors and formed a separate sect; they now make up around 10 per cent of the world's Muslim population. Shi'i sub-groups include Twelvers, Ja'fari, Ismaili and other communities. Shi'ism is the dominant religion in Iran, Azerbaijan. The Shi'i mourning phrase '*Ya Hassan, Ya Hussein*', chanted during the commemoration of the martyrdom of Ali's sons, was corrupted British colonial India into 'Hobson-Jobson' – itself the name for the Anglo-Indian argot which rendered regional speech according to English linguistic patterns.

Shifting Sands. All-purpose copout phrase designating analytic confusion and lack of any concrete understanding on the part of the writer of the country or issue involved. Like use of terms 'bazaar' and '*souq*', a vacuous term.

Shirt of Uthman. Repressive political order imposed by the *caliph* Mu'awiya after the assassination of his cousin Uthman, the third *caliph*, in 656 AD. Used in the Arab world after 11 September to justify increased suppression of dissent.

Shock and Awe. US military term, much heard in 2001–3, for the use of overwhelming military force against an enemy, in this case Iraq. Rather underestimated compliance of target population.

Shoah. Regular Hebrew word for 'catastrophe', i.e. what is called, variously, 'the Holocaust' or 'Judaeocide'. In contrast to 'Holocaust' the word is a straightforward neutral, secular, term without religious, mystical or providential overtones. Also the title of famous documentary film, made in the 1970s and released in 1985, by Claude Lanzmann. Cf. Arabicide, Genocide, Holocaust, Judaeocide, Politicide.

Shoe-Bomber. Term applied to Richard Reid, detained after attempting to blow up a Paris-Miami flight on 22 December 2001. Reid had hidden the powerful explosive triecetone triperoxide in his shoes. He said he had paid US$1,500 for the materials and had learnt how to make the bomb from the Internet. Triecetone triperoxide was used by the CIA in training Afghan *mujahidin*. French experts said Reid could have prepared the materials on his own. Israeli security officials insisted the explosive was similar to one used by Palestinians and showed a level of sophistication that suggested a co-conspirator. Reid himself, a British Muslim, came from London.

Silver Bullet. American expression for a one-off, complete or 'magical' solution. From both the Lone Ranger stories, as the hero's trademark (a reminder that life was as precious as silver) and the legend of the werewolf, according to which only a 'silver bullet' can slay the beast. Rather misused, to suggest invincibility of the enemy, as in the testimony by then-National Security Advisor Condoleezza Rice before the 9/11 Commission that there was no 'silver bullet' that could have prevented the attacks of 11 September.

Slam Dunk Case. From basketball; a forceful, definitive shot in which a player jumps up and pushes the ball down through the net. Phrase used by then-CIA Director George Tenet in December 2002 in reply to George W. Bush's question about the quality of intelligence on the likelihood of Iraqi WMD existing.

Smoking Gun. Term referring to some incontrovertible evidence for a matter under dispute or investigation. Misused as metaphor by Condoleezza Rice in calling for military action against Iraq before the threat became nuclear: 'We don't want the smoking gun to be a mushroom cloud.'

Sole Source Contracts. Euphemism for corrupt allocation of contracts, to friends and cronies. Applies to US defence and services contractor Halliburton in the aftermath of the 2003 Iraq war. According to the Government Accountability Office, war costs for fiscal year 2004 alone were US$12.3 billion above Pentagon estimates. Cf. Halliburton.

S.O.S. Acronym for 'Save Our Souls', a maritime distress signal; more recently used as 'Supporters Of *Shari'ah*' by preachers at London's Finsbury Park Mosque.

Soul of Islam. Misleading abstraction. Something for which the West and 'moderate' leaders in the Muslim world were reportedly 'battling' or 'struggling'. Beyond its dubious epistemological status, this term also implies what all existence, knowledge and common sense would contradict: that there existed, or could exist, one single or dominant opinion within the Muslim world. Distinct from 'Muslim public'. Cf. Arab Street.

Special Activities Division. Secret unit of the CIA consisting of small, irregular paramilitary groups of about half a dozen men, who do not wear military uniform. As of 2001, when the Division was being used for secret operations in Afghanistan, it was believed to have around 150 members consisting of fighters, pilots and specialists. The Division was equipped with helicopters, airplanes and the unmanned Predator drone.

Specifics-Free Warning. Announcement by US or other government of imminent terrorist attack, but without specification as to place or form.

Stand-up Kind of Guy. George W. Bush on Tony Blair at a press conference during latter's visit to Bush's Crawford, Texas ranch in April 2004.

State Sponsorship. Term used to assert or imply responsibility of states, usually anti-Western Middle Eastern states or, during the Cold War, the USSR and its allies, for the actions of terrorist groups. Much used after 11 September by those arguing that al-Qaʻida had the backing of significant Middle Eastern states beyond Afghanistan, notably Iran and/or Iraq and Syria. A much-mangled issue, as in a significant number of cases there was state backing for or facilitation of terrorist acts, and – in such cases as the German Democratic Republic – support for left-wing guerrillas in Europe itself.

Any balance sheet of state support for terrorism in regard to the Middle East over the two decades from 1980 would, however, have to include not only the role of the US's enemies (including Libya, which sent hundreds of tons of weapons to the IRA after the US bombing of Tripoli in 1986), but also the role of US's allies Saudi Arabia and Israel in backing illegal military and guerrilla groups (in Afghanistan and Lebanon) and that of the US itself which, in the 1980s under the guise of the 'Reagan Doctrine', funded right-wing terrorists in Angola and Nicaragua as well as Afghanistan.

Steganography. Concealment of secret messages in computer graphics or text, as allegedly practised by al-Qaʻida.

Stress Position. Forced sitting or squatting for up to four hours. One of a number of permissible interrogation techniques authorised by the US army in January 2003. Cf. Mild Noninjurious Physical Contact.

Suicide Bombing. Tactic used by terrorist and military groups in a number of countries during the twentieth century, notably the Japanese *kamikaze* ('divine wind') airplane pilots in World War II, Tamil Tiger guerrillas in Sri Lanka, Hizbullah in Lebanon and Islamists in Palestine. A distinction needs to be made between cases where this tactic is used against the soldiers of an enemy state (Japan, Lebanon) and where it is used against civilians associated with that state (Sri Lanka, Palestine, 11 September). The Arabic expression *'amaliyya istishhadiyya*, ('sacrificial operations') was commonly used in the 1990s. Those who dissented referred to such actions as *'amaliyya intihariyya* ('suicidal missions'). The Qur'an prohibits suicide, but not sacrifice in the cause of a just struggle.

Sunni. From *sunnah* (Arabic: literally, 'tradition'). The majority current in Islam, Sunnis number around 90 per cent of its followers. Less receptive to interpretation and innovation, Sunnis strongly adhere to texts and to the revival of political authority.

Sunni Triangle. Area of Iraq, bounded by Baghdad, Fallujah and Tikrit, where, in contrast to the rest of the country where either Kurds or Shi'is predominate, Sunni Arabs are in the majority. First coined by the Iraqi political scientist Dr Abbas Kelidar in 1975 to denote wider area of Mosul, Ratba and Baghdad.

Swastika. From Sanskrit *svastika* ('lucky charm'). Hooked cross found in many ancient traditions including Hinduism, adopted as symbol by the German National Socialist (Nazi) Party. Daubed on Jewish-owned buildings and on Jewish tombstones in postwar Europe, especially after 2000. Significantly, while European anti-Semitic ideas have found considerable diffusion in the modern Middle East, there has been no take-up of the *swastika* by those opposed to Israel.

Taghut. Qur'anic term for 'idol', object of pagan worship, to be destroyed by the faithful. Applied by modern Islamists, notably Khomeini, to describe political opponents (e.g. the Shah, Abol-Hassan Banisadr, Jimmy Carter, Saddam Hussein). Hence the generic term *taghuti* for the secular elite and its associated lifestyle. Wrongly used by many Arab writers to mean 'tyrant' (*taghin*).

Talib. Plural: *taliban*. Persian and Pashtu: literally, a religious student. Taken as the name of the movement, formed by recruits from Deobandi *madrasas* in Pakistan in 1994, which went on to capture Kabul in 1996 and control Afghanistan until 2001. Term contrasts with 'Students (*daneshjuan*) Following the Imam's Line', the group of Iranians who seized the American embassy in Tehran on 5 November 1979.

Tawhid wa Jihad. Militant anti-Western and anti-Shi'te Islamist group, active in Iraq in 2004, believed by be controlled by Abu Musab al-Zarqawi. In particular, denounced Arab and Muslim states such as Saudi Arabia and Pakistan that were considering sending forces to help stabilise the situation in Iraq.

Temara. Detention centre 10 miles south of Rabat, Morocco, used for secret holding and brutal interrogation of suspects in the war against terrorism. Run by the country's Directorate for Territorial Surveillance, an organisation without legal authority to detain. Denounced in an Amnesty International Report in July 2004. Following bomb attacks in Casablanca in May 2003, an estimated 7,000 people were arrested.

Terror Talk. Use by American teenagers of post-11 September slang, as in 'Ground Zero' to denote a messy bedroom; 'total *jihad*' for school punishment; 'so September 10' for a minor concern; the insult, 'your mama, Osama'; and 'Taliban', 'terrorist' and 'fundamentalist' as terms of abuse. (See 'In Times of Terror; Teens Talk the Talk', *International Herald Tribune*, 20 March 2002.)

Terrorism. Arabic: *irhab* (literally, 'intimidation'); Persian: *terorizm*. First used in 1795 to denote the terror of the French revolutionary state against its opponents, used in a similar way by the Bolsheviks, notably Leon Trotsky, to legitimate their actions. Had come in the second half of the twentieth century to refer almost exclusively to acts by opposition groups: assassinations; kidnapping; hijacking of planes (and occasionally ships and buses) with civilians; and bomb attacks on buildings and civilians in public places.

Theocracy. Literally, 'rule by God'. A misleading term, since what is meant is hierocracy, rule by clergy in the name of religion.

Third Temple. Name and goal of extreme, minoritarian Jewish movement seeking to rebuild the Temple on the site where the Second Temple, destroyed in 70 AD, once stood (now the site of the al-Aqsa mosque). In the 1940s this was a goal of Israel Eldad and the ideology of the terrorist group Lehi (also known as the Stern Gang). In 2004 an extreme group was reported as planning to crash a plane onto the al-Aqsa mosque as part of a campaign to destroy it and rebuild the Temple. One under-recognised problem about rebuilding the Temple is that were it to be reconstructed, it would be compulsory under Jewish law and tradition for the faithful to recommence mass animal sacrifices, as prescribed in the Bible.

Toothpicks. As in the observation by UN weapons inspector Hans Blix that the Iraqi *al-Samoud 2* missiles, which Baghdad had begun to destroy after 1998, were not 'toothpicks'.

Torah. Sacred text used by Israeli religious and nationalist forces to legitimate territorial and social policies, as in the slogan: 'There is no Israel without the Torah.' As with Muslim legal and political debates, this leaves entirely open the possibility of different interpretations and, indeed, of who is more or less entitled to interpret this text.

Tottering. Arabic: *mutamillmill*. Term used of 'regimes' denounced by Arab nationalists. Cf. Capitulationist, Defeatist, Wavering.

Toulouse. Southern French city, site of a major explosion of 300 tons of ammonium nitrate at an AZF factory, owned by TotalFinaElf, a few days after 11 September. Thirty people were killed and damage valued at 2 billion Euros was sustained. Three years after the event it was still not clear if this was an accident, or the work of an Algerian Islamist identified by the police as working in the factory.

Towelhead. Term of abuse for South Asians of any religion (including, of course, Sikhs, who wear turbans) in the US of the 1920s; now used more broadly of Muslims and Arabs.

Transfer/Transfer Out. Coded Israeli term, phrased in English, for possible expulsion of Palestinians from the West Bank and Gaza.

Transplantation Costs. Costs demanded by what are, under international law, illegal Israeli settlers in Gaza and the West Bank in return for an agreement to relocate within pre-1967 Israel.

Trenes de la Muerte. Spanish: 'Trains of Death'. Term for commuter trains blown up by terrorists in Madrid on 11 March 2004. Those killed were mainly poorer people from the southern suburbs of the city, going to work. The term has strange echoes, to a European ear, of the trains used to transport Jews to the Nazi death camps.

Triangle of Terror. One of a long line of pseudo-strategic geometric appellations used in the Cold War and afterwards by Western strategists, e.g. the Arc of Crisis. In this case, embodied in the title of book by Shaul Shay, *The Red Sea Terror Triangle: Sudan, Somalia, Yemen and Islamic Terror*.

Ulema. Arabic: someone proficient in *'ilm*, knowledge or science; plural of *'alim*, a man of learning. The equivalent of the clergy in Islam Also known as *mullahs*. Islam does not have an equivalent of the Christian sacrament of ordination, or a clear clerical hierarchy. Cf. *'Ilm, Mullahs*.

Umma. Arabic; word denoting the entire Muslim community. Mentioned sixty-two times in the Qur'an. The Qur'an suggests that in Paradise the Muslim *umma* will be a minority of all those present. In modern political discourse the term can denote the Arab world (*al-umma al-'arabiyya*) or the community of all Muslims. Contemporary usage suggests aspiration to unity of all members in one political community. Broader than the terms 'people', 'nation', 'country'. Also gives Arabic for 'internationalism' (*al-umamiyya*), nationalisation (*ta'mim*), and for the United Nations (*al-umam al-muttahida*). The same root is found in the Hebrew word *am* ('people'; 'nation').

Unlawful Passenger Behaviour. Term used by Russian aviation authorities to denote possible cause of twin airline crashes of 25 August 2004.

UNSCR 678. UN Security Council resolution of November 1990, authorising use of 'all necessary means' against Iraq; the legal and political basis for January 1991 war to drive Iraq out of Kuwait.

Venerated Cleric. Term used by Western media and diplomats to denote favoured Iraqi clergyman Ayatollah Ali al-Sistani, in contrast to terms used for his opponent and rival Murtada al-Sadr. Cf. Fiery Cleric, Renegade.

Viable. As in the significant and important diplomatic phrase 'viable Palestinian state'. This phrase is itself a concession, avoiding the issue of the *legitimate* Palestinian boundaries after the expansion of the Israeli state in 1967, but it too was open to multiple, and, in the end, ineffective redefinition. The general search for 'viable' state criteria was very much a feature of the earlier part of the twentieth century, since when states with almost no apparent objective basis for survival have, by dint of wit or accident, succeeded (Singapore, Monaco, Cayman Islands) while others, apparently endowed with natural criteria, have fared less well (Congo).

Vovchik. Russian; variant of the word *vahabobchik*, generically used of all Muslim political opposition in Afghanistan, Central Asia and the North Caucasus.

Wahhabism. Western term used of the official ideology of the Saudi state since its formation in 1902. More broadly, the movements supported, or allegedly supported, by Saudi Arabia. Founded by Muhammad ibn Abd al-Wahhab (1703–87). Followers of the strict Hanbali school of Islamic law, Wahhabism is one of the three main components of conservative Sunni Islam, along with the Muslim Brotherhood and the Deobandis. Ibn Abd al-Wahhab branded all who disagreed with him, including other Muslims and especially Shi'is as 'infidels' and declared *jihad* on them. In their 1802 conquest of Iraq, and in their revival during the early part of the twentieth century, they destroyed Shi'i shrines and tombs. The descendants of Ibn Abd al-Wahhab are today called the Al Sheikh ('the 'Family of the *Sheikh*'), in contrast to the politically dominant Al Saud. In Russia the term *vahabobchik* is now an all-purpose word for Muslim opposition groups. Cf. *Mowahhidun, Vovchik*.

War Against Islam. 'Campaign' or 'aggression' to which the Muslim world in general and the Arab world in particular are said to be subject. A paranoid fantasy. Cf. Against Islam, Anti-American.

War Against Terrorism. Analogous, in US political parlance, with the 'War Against Drugs' and the 'War Against Poverty'. Overstated rendering of campaign, policy or commitment.

Wavering. Arabic: *ha'ir*. A familiar term of derogation for states, classes (e.g. in earlier times, the petty bourgeoisie) and individuals deemed to be in contradiction with the speaker. Cf. Capitulationist, Defeatist, Tottering.

Weapons of Mass Destruction (WMD). Category of weapons covering nuclear, biological and chemical weapons, i.e. broader than nuclear weapons but beyond what were previously called 'conventional' weapons. First used by *The Times* in 1937 to describe the German bombing of Guernica, the term was revived in US arms control and official vocabulary of the 1970s. Despite the canonical usage of the abbreviation WMD, this term is far less precise than is often claimed. Many biological and chemical weapons are, while capable of wreaking terrible suffering on their specific targets at any one time, not capable of 'mass destruction'. Thus Professor Lawrence Freeman, writing of the confusion of chemical and biological weapons through use of this term: 'Their routine elision, which is now so ingrained as to be beyond remedy, encourages carelessness in public debate in failing to distinguish between systems that cause containable tragedies from those that would lead to the most unimaginable catastrophe.' (See *Survival. The IISS Quarterly*, vol. 46, no. 2, Summer 2004 p. 40 note 2.)

Whatever It Takes. Appeal by firefighters at the World Trade Center devastation of 11 September to George W. Bush on his visit after the attack, often cited by him in campaign speeches promising to make the American nation safer. Uncertain mandate in regard to respect for international law.

World War II Language. The global conflict of 1939–45 is the source of several terms used or revived in later conflicts, e.g. 'appeasers'; 'the Allies'; 'home front'; 'blitz'; 'Churchillian', etc.

YSP. Yemeni Socialist Party. Arabic: *al-hizb al-ishtiraki al-yamani*. Founded in June 1965 as the National Front for the Liberation of South Yemen. Came to power in South Yemen in November 1967 and transformed into the YSP in 1978. The only Arab regime to support Soviet-style 'scientific socialism'. Initially supported revolutionary movements against North Yemen, Oman, Ethiopia and Saudi Arabia. Weakened by factional disputes of 1969, 1978 and 1986 – this last involving several thousand casualties. Merged with conservative North Yemen in May 1990, and defeated in the inter-Yemeni civil war of April–July 1994. Retains semi-legal existence within Yemen.

Yorda. Hebrew: 'descent', i.e. emigration from Israel, in contrast to *aliya* ('ascent'). *Yordim* are Israelis who have left the country. In a land where statistics on everything else (except nuclear warheads) are plentiful, there is no official figure for the number of *yordim*. Estimates for 2004 suggested that up to 20 per cent of the population have left the country as a result of continued violence, political infighting and, by Western standards, a relatively low average income of around US$1,200 per month.

Zabib. Arabic: literally, 'raisin'. The mark on the forehead of a devout Muslim male indicating that he prays regularly and hence has acquired a mark at the point where his forehead touches the ground. Also known as '*dinar* of Allah'; *halat al-salah* ('the mark of prayer').

al-Zarqawi, Abu Musab. Jordanian Islamist, believed to be organiser of major Sunni-based military actions in Iraq in 2004, through *Tawhid wa Jihad* and other organisations. Laces anti-Western rhetoric with incitement to violence against Shi'is.

Zealot. Hebrew: *kana'im*. A religious or nationalist fanatic. Originally used of Jewish insurgents who rose against Roman rule in 70 AD, their defeat leading to the destruction of the Second Temple and the dispersal of the Jewish people. Associated in much Jewish tradition with needless violence and disputation.

Zion. A hill just south of the gates of Jerusalem, then applied to the city as a whole and later to the physical, but in some cases spiritual, land claimed by Jewish nationalists. A metonym, i.e. a part used to represent the whole.

Zionism. A form of modern Jewish nationalism, established at the 1897 World Zionist Conference in Basle, Switzerland, pioneered by Theodor Herzl in his 1896 book *Der Judenstaat* ('The State of the Jews'). Movement to establish a Jewish state in Palestine. In subsequent usage the term has acquired multiple meanings, that are best kept distinct:

(i)   that actual historical ideology and movement that, from 1897–1948, aimed to set up a Jewish state in Palestine;

(ii) since 1948, as general support and broad sympathy in both Israel itself and in the gentile world for that state and its continued existence;

(iii) in a pejorative sense, used by both European and North American fascists and anti-Semites and in much Middle Eastern rhetoric to denote a global, secretive, conspiratorial force; this fantastical racism purports to identify a worldwide ('Zionist') conspiracy as in the anti-Semitic forgery *The Protocols of the Elders of Zion*.

An earlier version of this Glossary appears in Two Hours that Shook the World, *London, Saqi, 2001. A small tribute to the late Raymond Williams, sociologist, historian and critic of culture and his* Keywords: A Vocabulary of Culture and Society, 1976. *Thanks also to the* Evening Standard, *23 October 2001; Cyril Glassé,* The Concise Encyclopaedia of Islam, *London, Stacey International, 1989;* The Shorter Oxford English Dictionary; *and Henry Yule and A. C. Burnell,* Hobson-Jobson. *Thanks to Jennifer Chapa, Lawrence Freedman and Dan Plesch for help with particular items.*

Index of Myths

Index of Names